ART is
Fundamental

ART IS Fundamental

Teaching the Elements and Principles of Art in Elementary School

Eileen S. Prince

CHICAGO
REVIEW
PRESS

Library of Congress Cataloging-in-Publication Data

Prince, Eileen S.,
    Art is fundamental : teaching the elements and principles of art in elementary school / by Eileen S. Prince.
            p. cm.
    Includes bibliographical references and index.
    ISBN 978-1-56976-216-5
    1. Art—Study and teaching (Elementary)—United States.   I. Title.
    N362.P748 2008
    372.5'044—dc22

                                                            2007048478

Cover design: Monica Baziuk
Cover images: Eileen S. Prince and the students at Sycamore School
Interior design and illustrations: Monica Baziuk
Interior artwork: Eileen S. Prince and the students at Sycamore School

© 2008 by Eileen S. Prince
All rights reserved
Published by Chicago Review Press, Incorporated
814 North Franklin Street
Chicago, Illinois 60610
ISBN 978-1-56976-216-5
Printed in the United States of America

Contents

Acknowledgments

ONCE AGAIN, I would like to thank all the administration, faculty, staff, parents, and students, past and present, at Sycamore School for their outstanding support throughout the years. I wish all art teachers could receive the encouragement and respect (and budget!) you have granted me. I am truly grateful.

Special thanks also go to:

Lauren Ditchley, my extremely talented assistant, who took all the photos for this book. Her cheerful and energetic demeanor make her a delight to work with, and her help in all areas is invaluable.

Betty Krebs and Courtney Henderson, the "fonts of all knowledge," without whose constant support none of us at Sycamore could teach or write books.

Larry Fletcher, John George, and B. J. Drewes, computer experts, who always manage to figure out the problem.

All the teachers, past and present, with whom I have worked and from whom I have learned.

Jerome Pohlen, my editor, for his encouragement and help.

Barbara Freeman, for 40 years of friendship and her countless hours of help on this book. If you understand the instructions, it's all due to her.

And once again, I want to thank my terrific family: my wonderful husband, Irwin, for his humor and support, and my incredibly brilliant and talented sons, Ben and Josh. (You too, Eric!) To all the rest of the family as well—you are the greatest!

Introduction

Before you start using the lesson plans in this book, I encourage you to read the entire volume. This is important for several reasons. You will gain a firm grasp of essential vocabulary and concepts that are embedded in the various lessons. You will be able to plan ahead for needed materials. You will have an opportunity to condense the material or delete or add projects to better serve your specific needs. And you will learn, in this section especially, some of the philosophy behind the curriculum and general strategies for implementing that philosophy. Parts of it may seem very basic, but remember that not every reader has had the same background. I have tried to include even small suggestions that might be helpful to a classroom teacher, homeschooler, or fledgling art instructor. Also, this is a curriculum I use with young children, and while it may easily be adapted to older students, and while I never intentionally "talk down" to my pupils, I do try to make it enjoyable and understandable for the target audience.

THREE ASPECTS of curriculum planning are equally important to a teacher: the content of the program, the rationale or philosophy behind that content, and the actual lesson plans that make the philosophy and content concrete and accessible to the student. In my first book, *Art Matters*, I presented all three, but I focused most heavily on rationale. While I certainly offered many lesson plans, they were not (with the exception of the art history projects) presented in complete or organized units. In this volume, I would like to suggest a specific curriculum for teaching the elements and principles of art. I use these lessons in grades one, two, and three at a school for academically gifted students, but they could easily be adapted to any level. (A visitor who observed my second graders reviewing vocabulary at the beginning of a class commented that she had been trying to get her sixth graders to understand those very concepts!) After reading the book, you might decide to substitute different lessons in certain spots. This is essentially an outline of the concepts I teach, with projects that I have used successfully to impart those concepts, but the projects are certainly not set in stone. I am always on the lookout for new and exciting ways to get my point across.

Those of you who are familiar with a discipline-based art education (DBAE) approach will no doubt notice that these are not typical DBAE units. Although my program is definitely discipline based, I do not follow the Getty model. I have the luxury of teaching grades one through eight, and while I certainly have turnover, my student population is relatively stable from year to year. Therefore, we study elements and principles for the first three years, art history for the next four years, and we focus on criticism and aesthetics in eighth grade. Of course, none of these areas is exclusive of the others. That is, we are always aware of questions of aesthetics and criticism, we almost always involve production in our culminating activities, we use historical and multicultural visual aids when discussing elements and principles, and we discuss elements and principles in our art history projects. However, each unit does not focus consistently on the four areas as in the Getty model. While I might hold up a poster of a Native American basket or a Chinese hanging scroll or a Picasso painting, in the early grades these are merely shown to demonstrate how artists use radial balance or value or shape. We usually don't study these works as works per se or the artists as artists until we begin the study of art history and can place them in historical and cultural context. Although I believe strongly in the structure of my program, I realize that many of you do not have the advantage of long-term association with your students or control over an eight-year curriculum, so at the end of appropriate lessons, I will offer suggestions for possible visual aids or artists that would illustrate the point. Accounts of these works and the artists can easily be found on the Internet, so I will not include that information here. If your situation allows, however, I strongly urge you to place art history units in historical context, so that students may see the cultural forces that influenced the rise and fall of styles and theories. I know that there is disagreement among some scholars about the way art history units should be arranged and how art history should be approached, but I do not intend to debate the topic here. (I discuss my philosophy in greater detail in my previous book.)

My units always involve other disciplines such as math, science, vocabulary, or language arts, so cross-curricular integration will not be a problem. You can tie these lessons in to the general curriculum in many ways. For example, in first grade, I do a color-mixing project that involves a story about a butterfly and incorporates symmetry. You might relate it to a math lesson on symmetry or Eric Carle's *The Very Hungry Caterpillar* or a science unit on insects.

It should also be fairly obvious how my curriculum relates to the national standards. Students who have been through my program (and who have paid attention!) have a solid art background, although they may cover concepts in a different sequence than your state standards. They have been exposed to a wide variety of artists, cultures, theories, methods, styles, and materials. I urge you to read *Art Matters* in order to fully understand the scope and sequence of my program.

Another feature of these lessons you might notice is that the time allotted to the various elements is not very even. That is, the study of color might entail 10 lesson plans while a unit on line might contain only two or three.

The reason for this seemingly inequitable approach is that the study of color involves far more uncommon vocabulary than the study of line. While lines might be thick or thin, wavy or straight, jagged or smooth, and so forth, most students can come up with these terms themselves. But they probably won't describe a color scheme as "monochromatic" or "complementary" unless they are introduced to these concepts.

One of the main reasons I teach elements and principles at this level is to develop vocabulary. Educational theory indicates that humans tend to notice things for which they have a word. Some sources even suggest that we cannot "see" something unless we have learned a term for the concept. The example usually given is that Eskimos have a wide variety of words for snow, each referring to a different quality. The implication is that if we knew all these words, we would each notice far more different types of snow than we currently perceive. While I don't claim to be an authority on perception, I definitely know from observation that students are far more likely to see things after they have studied the concept. For instance, a pupil will rarely discuss the fact that a painting is symmetrical or displays geometric shapes before they have learned what those terms mean. Thus, one of the most important aspects of this curriculum is to expand the students' perceptual skills through the development of vocabulary. An added benefit of this approach, especially for those of you who must justify the time and money spent on art class, is that this expanded vocabulary is not at all exclusive to art. As you shall see, I always try to explain the meanings of words in a variety of applications, and that expanded vocabulary is helpful on standardized tests.

Even if students don't verbalize the concepts they are learning, they can use them in a wide range of situations. Several years ago, one of the fourth grade teachers told me about a project she did in science each year that involved drawing certain rocks and minerals, matching the texture and color as closely as possible using crayons. (As I explained in *Art Matters*, nothing forces you to see something as completely as drawing or painting it.) She observed that students who had been in our art program automatically mixed colors to create appropriate results, while new students had difficulty solving the problem. Another student applied the concepts in a different way. When his mother asked him how he liked the arrangement of photographs she had created, he looked at it and offered the opinion that she had left "too much negative space." (She realized he was right.)

As I stated earlier, I use this curriculum in grades one, two, and three, therefore much of it is explained in very basic terms. Even older children with limited vocabulary skills might find this approach helpful, while other children with some exposure to the subject matter can skip a great deal of the introductory material. Only you know what is appropriate for your students. After reading a lesson, or group of lessons, you can decide how to condense or eliminate parts to serve your purposes. The projects themselves will need little or no adjustment, because a valid art project is self-individualizing. That is, given the same lesson, a first grader will complete it at one level, while a high schooler will (hopefully) produce something more sophisticated. (It is not unusual for one of the classroom assistants who accompany my lower-school students to art to ask if they can do the project with the children.) So you might skip a project entirely because your students already understand that concept, use it as is, or adapt it in any number of ways to suit your purposes. You can also rearrange units so that they might better integrate with the general curriculum, but make sure that you are not skipping necessary vocabulary, concepts, or skills if you rearrange things.

Don't assume your students have a certain level of understanding because of their age. It is not so much age as experience that will determine if some steps should be cut. For instance, in the first grade, I introduce proper paintbrush techniques in preparation for a painting that explores color. If your students are adept at using this tool, it is silly to waste time with that introductory lesson, but a seventh grader whose elementary school art program was cut may never have learned this basic skill.

You might also decide to eliminate projects in the interests of time. In the first grade curriculum, I present an introductory lesson that focuses on the concept that each artist is unique—that no two student works should look alike. You could adapt this lesson in a number of ways. You could simply explain that one of the reasons artists create is to share their view of the world, that no two people see the world in exactly the same way, and that you expect each of them to express his or her own view and not copy a neighbor's work. End of lesson. Or you could make your point by showing and discussing the introductory visual aids described in the lesson and forego the drawing assignment. Or you could ask older students to create, as homework, a drawing or painting or print that expresses the student's personal emotional state through the use of a tree image to stress the point. Several of the projects described in this volume could be done independently by older students, saving a great deal of class time. (Another way to save time is to use smaller paper. In most cases, a 9″ by 12″ background will serve as well as one that is 12″ by 18″.)

If you are shortening or adapting these lessons, I urge you once again to read the entire book before starting. You should then review the individual units in years one and two, because there is a certain amount of reinforcement that you might omit and certain projects from the second year that you might substitute for more basic projects in year one. For instance, after reading both units on color, you will see that Lesson 2 of the Second Year (as well as Lesson 2 of Third Year!) is mostly a verbal and visual reminder of ideas learned the previous year and might be skipped entirely in a one-semester middle school art program. Lesson 3 of year two essentially serves as a review of the concepts covered in Lessons 4, 5, 8, and 9 of year one (with reference to Lesson 10 as well), and might be used instead of those lessons in a one-year program. You might incorporate the practice of good paintbrush technique from Lessons 6 and 7 of year one into year two, Lesson 4, and merge the introduction of complementary colors into the project on color schemes. You will know which projects and approaches best suit your students.

The following curriculum reflects a school year of approximately 36 weeks where classes meet for 30 minutes twice each week. (Classes will occasionally be away on field trips.) While most of the projects take several periods, many first-year lessons are limited to one session. I have actually included a few extra projects in the first and second years so that you will have some flexibility. Be aware that the introduction and demonstration alone could take an entire period. Older students might proceed more quickly, or their works might be more complex and require even more periods. It will take some time for you to fine-tune your schedule. In the summaries that accompany each lesson, I will indicate the approximate amount of time we spend *as a class* on the project or exercise. Some students will finish more quickly and others will need to come back to it later. Also, while I recommend that the concepts and units follow this outline, the curriculum is not fixed. You might need to include a concept I have omitted or drop a topic entirely.

This is an extremely structured curriculum, and some art teachers prefer a freer approach to the subject. For some reason, people feel that the standards we apply to other studies don't pertain to art. Personally, I feel that the greatest freedom comes from mastery and knowledge—from understanding the possibilities. Students who follow my curriculum for several years are certainly as creative as their less "educated" counterparts, if not more so.

I had an experience several years ago that reinforced my attitude about this. A new student entered my school in eighth grade. Since my eighth graders have had three years of elements and principles, four years of art history, and a unit on aesthetics and criticism, this final year is relatively unstructured. Students are free to apply what they have learned or experiment with materials or styles they may not have had the opportunity to explore. One of the assignments I give is to create a still life. I have a variety of objects on a table that the students are free to use (or not), and the approach is completely up to them. The introduction is extremely brief, and during the year in question, the moment it was done, the students scattered and started to work. The new student simply sat. I didn't say anything that period, because the "thinking" stage is just as important as the "doing" stage, and I didn't want to intrude on the artistic process. But when she didn't begin doing anything at the beginning of the next period, I asked if she needed any help. She told me that she had never had a good art class, and she had no idea where to begin. She looked around the room at the other students all busily working and said in a rather envious voice that they all had ideas and seemed to know what to do. As any artist will tell you, getting started is half the battle. Your concept may change drastically as you progress, but having the confidence and knowledge to begin, and an idea of the possibilities, is crucial. If my goal is to draw a person seated in a chair but I have no concept of perspective, my results will probably fall short of my ambitions. Another aspect of structure is that students tend to feel more secure when they are given some parameters. Putting out some interesting materials and simply telling students to be creative is extremely intimidating to many children. Of course, the opposite approach—cookie-cutter lessons where everyone produces an identical product—is equally unacceptable.

Educators are aware that students have different learning styles, and that is why art is a practically perfect subject. In art class, you will discuss concepts verbally, write information and draw illustrations on the board, and allow students to manipulate materials, so every kind of learner should be able to access the concepts you are presenting. Another way to get your point across is through your own acting ability. Anything you can do to express yourself—hand gestures, facial expressions, dramatic vocal intonations during stories—will help students pay attention to and remember your words. Of course, every teacher has his or her own style, but boring, monotone presentations should not figure in any of them. Humor will always leave an impression, but at the very least, try to impart excitement about your subject. If *you* are not interested in color theory, why should your students be? People should teach from their passions whenever possible, but if you are teaching a subject because you must, not because you want to, please try to find it interesting first.

A final point about instructional styles: everyone, no matter how well they hear, gets some of their information by reading the lips of the speaker. I used to joke that I could hear better when I had my glasses on, and then I attended a conference session where I saw this concept illustrated. So even if all of your students have perfect hearing, which they don't, face them as much as possible when speaking. By the same token, stand at the desk farthest from the board to check how well a student seated there can see.

Finally, a word about budgets. I am extremely fortunate to work at a school where everyone values and supports the arts. My current facilities are outstanding, and I can purchase virtually any supply I want. But I have taught for well over 30 years, and my experiences have ranged from presenting "art on a cart," to sharing a room with instructors of other subjects, to my present embarrassment of riches. I am well aware that some art teachers are involved in challenging situations, and I will occasionally offer some solutions to particular problems. Unfortunately, no single book can be all things to all people, so while my curriculum, with one or two exceptions, does not require expensive materials, it does assume that you have access to sinks and that your students have crayons, markers, paper, pencils, glue, scissors, watercolors, and primary colors of tempera.

Getting Started

Classroom Strategies

The following are some fundamental principles you might want to consider before you start teaching. I have explained a little of my philosophy in the introduction, but these are some specific issues that I feel directly impact an art teacher's effectiveness in the classroom. The examples and stories I use here (and throughout the book) are those I also share with the children, unless otherwise noted. I rarely expect students to learn by osmosis. If I want to make a point, I'm clear about it, although I try to avoid talking down to my pupils.

Practical Considerations

Teaching art can be extremely stressful, especially if you have several messy classes in a single day. Unlike some curricula, my program is sequential, and students do not repeat projects. Thus, I cannot do one setup for a lesson that several grades are doing simultaneously, and I do not normally have different sections of the same grade back-to-back. The keys to avoiding a meltdown under these circumstances are organization, planning, and advance preparation. One of the advantages to my curriculum is that I know what to expect: I know what materials and setup I will need weeks in advance, I know the kinds of problems that might arise, and I know approximately how long the different processes take. Although I may repeat the same project for many years, my students never do—the task is always new to them. So while I am constantly on the lookout for better ways to convey an idea, once I find a project that teaches the concept enjoyably, fits my time frame, and is appropriate to the students' age level, I usually stick with it. And while there are always setup and procedural concerns specific to each project, there are many general measures you can take to make your life easier. The following suggestions may not be workable for everyone, but the underlying theories might be helpful.

Room Arrangement

If it is at all possible, it will cut down on preparation time a great deal if you can group your desks or use actual large tables. My 24 desks are two feet deep and three feet wide, and I have them arranged in groups of six, creating four-by-nine-foot tables. Years ago, my art students sat at eight-foot folding banquet tables. This clustering of students allows for sharing of supplies and requires far fewer water buckets, tempera paint cups, and so forth. If you are teaching in your regular classroom and have no space for extra tables, you might have the students rearrange their desks for art, if possible.

In the center of each cluster, I have a basket of basic supplies. Since my tables can accommodate six students, each basket contains six boxes of crayons (24-count), six boxes of regular markers, six art gum erasers, six scissors, six glue sticks, a plastic box filled with colored pencils, and 8 to 10 regular pencils. I also throw in a couple of small plastic crayon/pencil sharpeners, although we have two electric sharpeners in the room as well. My baskets are roughly 10″ by 16″ plastic ones with handles, the kind you might find in the storage section of any discount store. They can easily be removed for certain projects, but for most of our lessons they make preparation a breeze. I find this approach preferable to students bringing individual supplies from their own classroom in personal boxes. If your school's budget does not stretch to duplicate supplies for the art room (assuming you have an art room), consider carrying such baskets back and forth.

You will need to spend some time keeping the baskets tidy. If you use crayons in tuck boxes, I recommend taping the bottom of the boxes to avoid accidents. If your budget allows, buy enough crayons to replace the sets completely two or three times a year. Regardless, encourage students to put the colors back properly. Also, it is a good idea to purchase several one-color refill boxes of black, white, red, yellow, and blue. Find a place to keep old crayons. You can use them to replace lost or broken ones from the newer boxes.

Water and Cleanup

When water is required for a project like painting, I prefer large containers rather than the small individual pans that were in vogue when I was young. The terrific lady who runs the lunch program at our school is very kind about saving me the white plastic buckets that many of her supplies come in. These hold one to two quarts of water, stack nicely for storage, cost nothing, and are easily replaced. I put two on each of my tables, so that all six students may reach one. If I know that I will be using water for a project that day, I simply fill the containers first thing in the morning and leave them in or near the sink. The students empty and rinse them after the lesson. If you have no water in your room, you might put a very large plastic container of water somewhere and allow students to scoop water into their own containers and dump the dirty water there when done.

Several years ago, our school put paper towel dispensers in each room, the kind that use white, perforated rolls, but I asked them to skip my classes. Instead, the custodian supplies me with cartons of brown, tri-fold, individual towels that I can place in stacks on the tables and on the counters near the sinks, where my smaller students can reach them more easily. I bought plastic shoe boxes for the ones near the sinks, so that watery messes don't cause us to waste any.

Near my sinks, I also have four large plastic buckets with handles. Each bucket contains six large sponges. If a project is particularly messy, I simply run a little water in each bucket to dampen the sponges, place a bucket on each of the tables, and let the children clean up. Using good sponges is a little pricy—perhaps your custodial department will supply you with materials.

Visual Aids

If possible, it is a good idea to have some visual aids on permanent display. I not only have sets of posters that generally explain the elements and principles of art, I have also put up some examples that I find helpful when discussing specific concepts. Having them constantly on view not only saves time, but it allows the children to use them as reminders from year to year. For instance, I have a copy of a painting that depicts a prince in metal armor wearing a velvet cape lined with fur and lace at his throat. It includes satin, carved wood, hair, and a variety of other textures, and I use it to illustrate how artists can create the illusion of texture. When I return to it from time to time, the students remember the concept.

Obviously, you will need a large, easily visible color wheel. You can make your own, download one off the Web and enlarge it, or order a nice one from an art supply catalog. These come in a wide variety of formats. Older students can be extremely creative if you have them make their own.

You will also need some kind of storage for the visual aids you use only for particular lessons. Old calendars are a wonderful source of pictures, and of course the Internet can supply you with almost any visual you need.

A very basic color wheel. (See color insert)

Materials

In some cases, it does not matter which brand of materials you use, but in others, it can make a big difference. Certain watercolors have awful brushes or extremely weak pigments, which makes using them very frustrating. I have found over the last few years that Prang has maintained a nice quality watercolor for the price. I like Crayola crayons in packs of 24, because, in spite of the silly names they have given some of the hues, the box does contain an actual 18-color color wheel. It is a good idea to check your supplies immediately when the order comes in each year to make sure the manufacturers have not degraded the quality substantially in order to keep costs down.

Rules

After I introduce myself on the first day of each year, I immediately explain the rules for art class. Most of these are pretty generic, reflecting what goes on in other rooms, and you will no doubt have a list of your own. They involve such issues as safety, behavior, bathroom procedures, and being respectful when someone is speaking, and I get through them pretty quickly. There is one rule, however, I discuss at some length, and that is "We never touch anyone else's artwork." I explain that I must know whose work I'm evaluating. Let's say Jenny draws the best horses in first grade and Johnny wants a horse on his paper. Jenny may show Johnny how to draw a horse, but she may not draw it for him on his project. If I missed seeing her draw on Johnny's paper, I might fill Johnny's grade card with a discussion of how well he draws horses, and that would not be true. This, of course, has much greater implications in upper grades.

That is one reason for the rule. Another (extremely important) aspect is that no student may mark on another pupil's paper in anger. If a student accidentally drips or spatters something on a neighbor's project, the victim may *not* retaliate by making marks of any kind on the offender's paper. "How would you feel," I ask my class, "if you had worked hard on a piece for the whole period (or longer) and someone purposely ruined it? If someone causes a problem with your project, accidentally or on purpose, simply come to me and I will fix it. Accidents happen, although they will happen a lot less if everyone follows the instructions."

Actually, I get pretty intense about the idea of purposeful destruction in any form. Artists are creators. I discuss the fact that anyone can destroy something, but it takes someone special to create. This discussion of destruction applies to materials as well as projects.

Another rule I find very helpful is "Don't touch anything on the tables until you are given permission." Not only is it rude, distracting, and sometimes noisy to be fiddling with things while someone is talking, but students can disarrange items you have set out in a particular way before you have time to explain a concept.

One other subject I discuss on the first day of class is what we mean by "doing" art. I consider that we are doing art from the time we enter the classroom. I am very lucky that most of my students have been at my school since kindergarten or earlier and have therefore already experienced a wonderful early childhood art program that involves looking and listening as much as doing. My pupils don't expect to walk in the door and immediately start drawing, painting, or sculpting. I still get a student or two each year who will interrupt a wonderful discovery session with the question, "When are we going to start doing art?" So I think it is only fair to warn students that sometimes—not most of the time, but on several occasions—we will spend a period just looking and talking, and that will count as "doing" art, too.

Finally, when we are doing art, I allow my students to chat. The rule is that you may talk quietly with your neighbors as long as you are working. If the room gets too noisy, I know that the children are talking more than working. If a reminder or two doesn't do the job, that class might lose its talking privileges. Only you will know how much freedom your class can handle, but I must admit I find a totally silent art room somewhat eerie.

Demonstrations

As you will see, I usually present very specific demonstrations of procedures in the early grades. Even college teachers offer step-by-step instructions for new techniques. I would like to offer three suggestions about demonstrations.

First, be sure you are extremely comfortable with the project before you present it to others. Even some of the activities we do with young children are tricky if you are unfamiliar with them. Also, materials change over the years. School papers and pigments have gotten steadily worse in quality, and projects don't always work the same way they used to. If you are in any doubt at all, practice before you teach.

Also, a brief word about color theory. When an artist says, "Blue and yellow make green," that is a generality. Actually, there are two sets (or more) of primaries: warm and cool. The violet you get by mixing a warm red with a cool blue is not the same as the one you get by mixing a cool red with a warm blue. This is why I often recommend using magenta and turquoise in demonstrations and another reason you need to practice and be prepared before you do them. I discuss this briefly with my classes. If you are working with older students, you might want to study this and go into it at more length.

Second, begin with a thorough, start-to-finish demonstration, then remind students of each step along the way. Some people learn sequentially and others need to see the entire process in order to understand what you are saying.

The third aspect of demonstrations that you will want to consider is copying. When I illustrate a process, I always explain to my class that their images should not look like mine, but that admonition is not always sufficient. If I see a student using similar elements, I will talk to them about making sure their project looks very different before it is finished. One way I discourage copying is to use abstract shapes or forms, but when I draw realistically, I use the same image over and over for my demonstrations, until it is simply too boring to copy. I use a house, ground, a tree, a mountain, a cloud, and a sun, or some combination of those, until it becomes a class joke. That does not mean that a student cannot draw a house or a tree as well, only that their results should be personal. You might find some combination of images that work for you or a different method entirely, but try to discourage copying.

Describing Folds

There are three basic types of folds we use in art class. If you fold a simple 8½″ by 11″ piece of paper in half so that each half measures 8½″ by 5½″, we call this type of division a "hamburger" fold. Were you to fold the piece in half the long and narrow way, that would be a "hot dog" fold, and when you fold a square piece of paper on the diagonal, that's a "taco" fold. When you fold a piece of paper, the part that sticks up is called the "mountain" of the fold, and the other side is called the "valley." These terms help the children follow the instructions more easily.

Class Review

Because I give very few tests during my eight-year program, I rely heavily on repetition to help my students remember the material. I usually achieve this repetition through a review at the beginning of each class. Such an exercise is especially important when a project continues for more than one period, in order to remind students of the instructions and the concepts being covered, so even if you do plan to test your students, reviews can be helpful. These brief sessions at the beginning of the period have the added advantage of settling the students and helping them focus on the subject at hand. They also create a certain consistency for the children. As you read the book, you will find suggested formats for these reviews, and important review topics are included with each lesson.

Of course, throughout this question and answer period, I try to call on as many different children as possible and to be fair to both genders. After calling on a student, I give him or her several seconds to answer. Even some children who know the material need time to collect their thoughts. When a student answers correctly, I reward that success with a smile and some congratulatory word like "great" or "excellent," but I try not to make a big deal out of wrong answers, although I do acknowledge the mistake. A simple "nope," or "That's a great example, but not a definition," is more than enough, and if I feel she will be more successful, I will often ask if the child would like to try again. The point of all this is that I try to keep the pressure to a minimum. If you make a mistake, you learn from it and move on. I want my students to feel free to take a chance. After all, that's what art class is all about. As I frequently remind my class, art is constant decision making, and we don't always make the right choice.

Just a brief clarification: there is a difference between taking a chance on answering a new question or making a legitimate mistake, and giving an answer that indicates you have not been paying attention for the last few days or have completely missed the point. In spite of certain modern philosophies about this, I have no trouble identifying a wrong answer as such, I just do it with a minimum of fuss and attention.

Collecting and Passing Back Projects

As you will see, for most projects, names go on the back in pencil. I will point out exceptions in the instructions. Wet projects should be put on a drying rack and need identification, but in all cases, having one's name on the piece is very important. Every child has a portfolio and each class has a "cubby" where their portfolios are stacked. Even my first graders have easy access to their work.

In my upper grades, students are responsible for filing ongoing projects in their portfolios and retrieving them to work on. With younger children, you could start each period by passing out portfolios and end it by having the students file their projects in them, but I usually don't do that. I like to discuss each project with the student as I pass it back, even if it's only a comment like "You're doing great!" I might OK a student's advance to the next step, or catch a problem that I missed the previous period. It saves time to simply collect the current projects at the end of the period, stack them, and place the stack on top of that group's portfolios. We have several "file and free" periods during the year to let students catch up. If a student completes a project while his classmates are still working, he usually files it in his portfolio and may use the remaining time to finish earlier pieces. When there are small, loose pieces at cleanup time, you might create the kind of "sandwich" discussed in Lesson 23 of the first year, or wrap the whole stack in a large piece of paper as I describe in Lesson 7 of the third year.

When one of the steps in a process involves watercolors or texture plates or oil pastels, I might set out the projects before the students come in, putting pieces that are not yet ready for those materials at different tables from those that are. I usually differentiate between "wet" and "dry" tables.

Dealing with Mistakes in Art

To a great extent, the artistic process is like the scientific process. Artists have to be prepared for their "hypotheses" to be disproved—sometimes the color or shape or approach they thought would work is simply not successful, and they have to try again. Every artist has a closet filled with "mistakes." Successful artists are the ones who keep trying. My students need to feel free to take (appropriate) risks.

I want to add a small explanation here. I always expect students to carefully follow directions when we are doing a project where instructions are involved. In middle school, for instance, I teach my classes perspective, and those introductory lessons are not really open to creative interpretations. One of the reasons Escher could produce such wonderful optical illusions by subverting perspective was that he understood the rules so thoroughly. I explain that to my students, and I always tell them that once they have learned perspective, they need never use it again in their personal work, but simply understanding it will inform that work. There is a difference between choices based on knowledge and those based on ignorance. There is also a difference between class exercises and true art. Learning to use a paintbrush properly is an exercise we practice so that poor technique will not inhibit our ability to produce art. Failing to follow instructions can actually make the project impossible. If you cut the slits for a paper weaving on the wrong end of the "loom," you can't weave on it. So even in first grade, I will correct a student who is following instructions poorly. I am simply gentler with my younger students until they are comfortable with such correction.

When the instructions include a directive such as "Don't make any tiny shapes," there is always a little wiggle room. If the student has a wonderful composition that includes one or two tiny shapes, I will usually let that pass. By and large, I'm concerned with whether the design will work for the given project and how well the student is following instructions *generally*.

I give only three tests in my eight grades: a vocabulary test in third grade, a perspective test in sixth, and another vocabulary test for review in eighth grade before students graduate. I am a lot less understanding about poor results in my eighth grade classes, but I always allow anyone who wants to take a retest to do so. My purpose in giving a test is to have the students remember certain vocabulary or prove to me they fully understand a concept, and I appreciate a child who wants to improve.

So while I can be pretty stern about some things in art class, I try to be very accepting of honest mistakes. (See "General Guidelines for Judging Student Work," page 12.)

Touching Student Work

Knowing when and how to touch student work can be very tricky. Some teachers would advise you never to do it at all, and others do it far too frequently and intrusively. My general attitude is that "a picture is worth a thousand words." If, after my visual demonstration on the board and several verbal suggestions about her piece, Jill is still having trouble understanding my point, I might draw directly on her paper. In lower grades, this usually involves showing students how to use lines to break up backgrounds when they try to accomplish this by adding more and more shapes. (This refers to projects where a form of tessellation is called for.) If I am trying to get them to draw a larger image, I will usually use a separate piece of paper and copy what they have done in a larger format to show them the difference, then let them try again. A lot depends on the purpose of the project. It is their job to create the image. As you will see, this curriculum does not involve showing a student a particular way to draw a house or tree or rabbit, and even observational drawing allows a student the opportunity to develop his or her own style. Indeed, it would defeat the purpose of observational drawing if I showed exactly how to draw that plant or person. However, it is my job to teach students about composition, and this is where I might add a line or two to their works. Technique is another area where I might need to touch the project to help. A student who continues to scrub with a paintbrush after a demonstration and repeated remonstrances might benefit from seeing the correct approach used in a stroke or two on his paper. The aim is to help the student to better express himself, not to do the project for him, but art is ultimately a visual exercise, and it may be impossible to verbally get your point across.

Slower/Faster Students

Students keep their projects in portfolios, so they are available for work after the class has moved on. (See First Year, Lesson 1.) I do not advance to the next lesson as soon as the quickest student has finished, nor do I wait for the slowest child. Allotment of class periods is based upon the time it takes the majority of students to finish the work. If a student completes her project before the rest are done, she has several choices. She may work on unfinished pieces from her portfolio, create a "free" drawing, tackle a game or puzzle in the room, or work on the computer. If a student is not finished when the class moves on, the project will be in his portfolio, and he can work on it during "file and free" periods (see First Year, Lesson 13), or when he completes a subsequent project early.

General Drawing Suggestions

When you are starting a project, it is frequently reassuring to students to allow them to start with pencil. In fact, for some lessons, this will be a requirement so that you can catch problems before they are indelible. However, in certain projects, I would encourage the student to work directly in marker or crayon, because otherwise they will never progress to the color stage. These occur mostly in first grade, and include drawings that will only last one period, like

First Year, Lesson 2, or the First Year seasonal drawings. These will be obvious as you read through the curriculum.

One of the most beneficial exercises for students is drawing from reality—what we call observational drawing. This type of work has been shown to have a positive effect on other aspects of the general curriculum. Several of the projects in this book are appropriate for observational drawing, and that will be noted in the instructions. The student can simply draw the environment around them, other students, or a still life that you have created, such as a grouping of potted plants. If students go outside to sketch, they will probably need drawing boards to support their paper. These can easily be made by cutting sides of corrugated boxes into rectangles about 12″ by 18″ or a little bigger.

Integrating Subjects Across the Curriculum

I believe very strongly in weaving art into the general curriculum. My first book, *Art Matters*, deals with this topic at great length, so I will discuss it only briefly here. I am in favor of integrating art, but not in a way that makes it a cute, culminating activity for the "real" curriculum. I believe that every subject should be taught with as many connections as possible, so it is important to relate art to math and science and literature and history. It is also important to relate science to math and literature and history and art. As I stated in the introduction, my projects almost always connect to the general curriculum in some way, even if it is only through vocabulary words. My youngest students do lessons that relate to geometry, symmetry, tessellation, physics of light, social studies, and storytelling, among other topics, but there are many ways to integrate the projects with classroom studies. The easiest is subject matter. When you have passed out the paper and students are deciding what to draw, you might simply refer to what they are studying in their other classes. Insects, transportation, buildings, the solar system, Native Americans, state history, or plants all offer countless ideas for images, and several topics lend themselves to observational drawing as well.

Displaying Student Work

Most schools have some sort of spring art show or creative arts festival during the year. I also try to keep general displays on the hall walls. How you present student work will depend on your space and budget. When I started teaching art, I was unable to have ongoing displays, and my spring show consisted of placing the art on tables and chairs in the gym for one evening. My current facility has wonderful wall space, and I fill it as much as possible. If time is a factor, you could simply put up unmounted, unlabelled work as it is finished, with the understanding that selected works will be mounted and labeled for the more formal show.

These displays serve several purposes. First, since the students don't take their projects home until the end of the year, it allows the parents to see that their children are, in fact, working in art class. Second, the displays are educational. I never put up a group of projects without a small sign that explains the purpose of the lesson. It might be entitled "Mixing Primaries" and read something like, "It is hard to believe that the second graders made these beautiful colors using only red, yellow, and blue crayons." Third, because the projects are generally terrific, they impress parents, administrators, and guests. When people visit the building, their first impression is frequently created by the children's artwork, and when this gets great comments from those visitors, it encourages the administration to support the program. Finally, of course, the children are delighted and proud to have their art displayed. While I don't display every student's work every time, I try to make sure everyone has at least one piece of work included over the course of the year, if possible. Obviously, I do not hang sloppy or mostly unfinished work. I will not reward a student who does not make a sincere effort, and it might embarrass a student if his or her work is noticeably inferior. Also, I don't make a display for every project we do.

Earlier in my career, I spent a spring break mounting and labeling work for the spring show. Since this eventually totaled some 700 pieces, I either came into the building over vacation to hang them or arrived at school an hour or so early for several days after break and/or stayed late to accomplish this. Finally, I learned to mount and label each piece as it went up for general display, so I had much less work to do over vacation. But time was also a factor for this approach, and I couldn't change displays as frequently as I wanted. Now that I have an assistant, much more work gets displayed, and neither of us is overwhelmed when spring rolls around. When a general display comes down, the pieces can be refiled in the portfolios or simply set aside for the spring show. Perhaps you have a parent or two who would volunteer to help you.

I have mounted projects in a number of ways. I have cut "window-frame" mats from poster board and saved them from year to year. Most of the projects are standard size: 12″ by 18″ or 9″ by 12″, so you simply use a mat knife to create an opening a little smaller in one half of a piece of poster board and use masking tape to apply the art from behind. But the easiest way to mount art is to simply center it and staple it on the front of a solid half sheet of poster board. I have found that stapling is the least damaging of the methods I have tried, and the pieces are secure—they won't fall off the mount. For 9″ by 12″ works, I usually use 12″ by 18″ construction paper as the mat. (If cost is a great factor, you might keep all projects as small as possible.) Even before we had tackable walls, I just stapled the pieces up using an electric stapler, but there are many new products out there if this is a problem.

I use a computer program that creates and stores labels, and I print them on 1″ by 4″ gummed blanks, the kind that come in sheets of 20. When cost was more of a factor, I printed them on regular paper, cut them out, and glued them on by hand. Here is an example of one of my labels.

```
NAME_____
CONCEPT: GEOMETRIC SHAPE
```

I simply run a page or two, fill in the names I need, peel, and stick one on the lower-right-hand corner of the mat. I never put anything on the artwork itself. If you are saving your mats, you could use the kind of glue that makes "sticky notes," or simply put the new label over an old one.

I have special places I put each grade for the spring show, but I always have signs so that spectators will know what grade level they are viewing and what overall concepts are represented, something like "Grade One: Focus on Elements." The labels will offer more specific information. Most of the work will already be mounted from previous displays, but I always go through portfolios for any nice pieces that might not have been chosen before. In lower grades, every child has at least one work on display, while the average child has two or three. Some teachers have the students go through their portfolios and select their favorites.

General Guidelines for Judging Student Work

There are at least two different types of judgment involved in student projects. There is the constant feedback we give our students as they work on a piece and the more formal grade or final verdict we are usually required to submit for report cards. I feel it is important to discuss both kinds of assessment, even if they are, as in my classes, closely related.

I know that some people feel that we should never judge student art, but I will admit I find that attitude incomprehensible. Do these people accept everything the student does without comment? Do they display every student's work for every project? If not, then how do they choose? Surely judgment is involved somewhere. I would like to elaborate on this concept, because I feel it goes to the heart of art education.

For some reason, many people apply different standards to visual arts than they do to performing arts. We don't assume that teaching a child to read music or use proper fingering on an instrument will inhibit a child's musical creativity. Certainly, few of us listen to children in first grade (or above) banging randomly and atonally on a piano and compliment them on the beautiful music they are making. By first grade, we expect them to sing along with the other children in the choir performance, perform the prescribed steps in the dance recital, and recite the appropriate lines in the class play. But we are told that we must joyfully accept their sloppiest scribbles in art class lest we damage their self-esteem. Needless to say, I totally disagree with that philosophy.

While I would be delighted to forego the report card kind of assessment, my job is to help my students learn new skills and concepts and to improve those they have already covered. If I fail to point out areas that I feel need improvement, how will my students grow? If I don't model good critiquing practices, how will they internalize that approach and become good critics (in the best sense of that term) themselves? While I would never discuss student work in a way that demeans the pupil, I will tell even a first grader if I feel his or her project has problems. I believe there are ways to do this that don't result in hurt feelings or diminished effort, although of course there are children who can't take criticism at all, no matter how gentle.

Judging student art—or any art, for that matter—is a difficult process. I believe that we must first define what we mean by the term "art."

I have studied (and taught) this subject for most of my life, and I have never found a definition that works for me in every case. In the last few years, I have relied most heavily on Richard L. Anderson's book, *Calliope's Sisters*, in which he concludes that art is "culturally significant content, skillfully encoded in an affective, sensuous medium." In some cases, even young students are capable of producing this concept of art, but I believe there is a difference between an exercise or assignment, and true art. I mentioned this briefly in the section on "Dealing with Mistakes in Art" (page 7).

While I rarely dictate subject matter in these early classes, the student is not totally free in the creation of the work. As you will see, there is always a point to the lesson, such as learning the difference between organic and geometric shapes or exploring the effects of distortion. (One might argue that a portrait painter or commissioned artist also works under certain constraints, but that is a different issue.) For that reason alone, I would be reluctant to judge this type of student work in exactly the same way I judge professional or even later student pieces. There are many similarities, however. In most cases, I refer to what I call "the four C's"—craftsmanship, comprehension, creativity, and composition—and effort.

When I look at a completed work, one of the first qualities that I notice is craftsmanship—that is, how well the artist controlled the materials. I will notice it more if it is exceptionally nice or exceptionally poor. It is usually obvious when a child has chosen a more expressive style or simply not made the effort to work carefully. As I discuss at length in Lesson 36 of the First Year curriculum, "thinking outside the box" is not the same as "coloring outside the lines." While some students have actual motor control issues, for most children, craftsmanship is simply a matter of effort. In either case, the problem requires attention. Art is a means of visual communication. If the messiness of a work interferes with its message—if it is not part of the story, like lines for wind that might cut through a tree, or purposeful strokes that are meant to add movement to an abstract piece—then that problem needs to be corrected. I usually urge the child to slow down and work more carefully. I frequently make statements in class like, "This is not a race, it's an art project," or "I would rather see a project partly done beautifully than finished but a mess."

Composition is another striking quality. Some students simply have a feel for filling the page in an aesthetically pleasing way, and for others it is a real struggle. We talk a lot about leaving too much negative space in a piece. While I don't actually "mark down" for this unless it was the point of the lesson, good design does enhance a project, and I will frequently include a comment on a report card to the effect that "Alex has a nice feel for composition."

"Comprehension" refers to how well the child got the point. If the entire purpose of the lesson was to see the effect of complementary (opposite) colors and a student uses analogous colors instead, then he or she obviously didn't comprehend the concept. When this happens, I will usually inform the parent that "Pat needs to listen carefully to instructions."

I use "creativity" to refer to that quality of an artwork that sets it apart from the others in the class. At a school for gifted children, it is not at all unusual for most of the finished projects to exhibit nice craftsmanship, good composition, and fine comprehension. This result is intensified by the class critiquing process I describe later. But there will always be those pieces that simply stand out because of a unique approach. This might be unusual imagery, a sophisticated eye for color, or simply a certain *je ne sais quoi* that other art teachers would recognize as well. Sometimes it is a product of observational skills, although in the early years it is hard to decide if these results are determined primarily by artistic or intellectual giftedness. (A great deal of *Art Matters* is based on the premise that the two are closely related.)

Two examples come to mind. At my previous school, I taught kindergarten in addition to grades one through eight. One of the students in that class drew a picture of children on a playground on a rainy day. He drew puddles on the ground, and one of the puddles reflected the images next to it perfectly. And just this year, a first grader's painting displayed a table in a diner. The viewer is inside the diner, looking across the table to the front windows. Not only are the utensils on the table in the correct position for our perspective, but the word "open" on the front window is backward, so that the people on the street will see it properly. Whether such observational skills are the result of intellectual or artistic talent, they are certainly assets to a student who might choose to major in art. (They would also benefit a writer, a scientist, or a police officer.)

Finally—and perhaps most importantly—I look for sincere effort. Such effort goes beyond "doing." It implies that the student pays attention to instructions, participates in reviews, and tries his or her very best on projects. When students make such an effort, issues of comprehension and craftsmanship usually don't arise. The vast majority of projects displaying poor craftsmanship are the results of rushing. When a child has actual difficulties with motor control, but she gives art her best effort, she will always receive a good grade. Since all of my students are required to take art, it would be unfair of me to base my judgment on artistic ability, and even that ability is not always evident in a finished project. I have very young students who take the process of creating art extremely seriously, who think quite carefully about each choice they make, but as I stated previously, artistic choices are not always successful.

My school has recently adopted a new grading system in the lower grades for "Specials" teachers (this includes those who teach physical education, music, Spanish, computer skills, and art). Many of you may be familiar with this system, and I have found it very useful. The student receives either a one, two, three, or four in each of three categories: performance, effort, and behavior. A "three" implies that the student has successfully fulfilled all the (admittedly rigorous) class requirements, a "two" suggests that a student is on the right track toward success but not quite there yet, and a "one" informs the parents that the child has a great deal of work to do. Of course, numbers are accompanied by explanations where necessary. "Fours" are reserved for students who show exceptional ability in an area. This might be reflected in the kind of unique project noted previously (performance), being especially kind or helpful to another student (behavior), or demonstrating a profound love of the artistic process (effort). Parents are informed that a three is an excellent mark and warned not to expect fours as a matter of course.

I like this format, because it allows me to acknowledge that a student is doing everything I ask, and doing it well, while still letting me recognize those who go above and beyond. Most of my students make threes, primarily because of the second type of critiquing I mentioned, the constant discussion of ongoing work.

Like most art teachers, once the children have begun work on a project, I roam around the tables observing their progress or answering questions that might arise. As I do so, I offer words of praise and encouragement *when they are justified.* Before I continue, allow me to step up onto my soapbox for just a moment. I have referred to this issue once already, and those of you who read *Art Matters* will find the following words familiar, but I feel this subject is so fundamental to education in general and art education in particular, it cannot be stressed too strongly.

We hear a great deal in today's classroom about self-esteem, and teachers are taught that one of the most important aspects of affective education is the development of the student's feeling of self worth. While I am totally in agreement with this sentiment, I think many parents and teachers are laboring under a misconception about how to help children improve this facet of their personalities, and this misconception has had an almost disastrous effect on art education. Because so many people view art class, at least at the elementary level, simply as a therapy or play period without significant content or standards, they feel it is a good place to praise virtually anything a student produces without regard to true merit. I have already mentioned some teachers' reluctance to critique student artwork for fear that such analysis might diminish a child's self-esteem. Imagine this theory being applied to piano lessons or math homework. I believe this is a self-defeating practice on many levels.

In the first place, you cannot confer self-esteem on someone simply by telling them how wonderful they are if they see no personal evidence to support your assertion. A pupil who rarely solves a math problem correctly is not going to believe that he is a terrific math student, no matter how many times you tell him that he is. We might fairly laud his effort and work ethic but not his product. And while I suppose that a child bombarded from birth with protestations of her wonderfulness might come to believe it after a while, what real service does that do her? Of course I believe in general praise that offers the child acceptance as a human worthy of respect, and naturally I do not advocate belittling or denigrating remarks. But true feelings of self-worth come when we meet and overcome obstacles. Art classes, like any other, need challenging curricula that the children can master if they work hard.

Secondly, children are not stupid. They know when they are being patronized. "Dumbing down" the curriculum only denies them skills they will need in later life without providing the self-esteem boost such an action is theoretically designed to supply, and simply offering indiscriminate praise is just as bad. If two of my students are trying to draw a horse realistically, and one child's work looks like a Kentucky Derby winner while the other resembles a lobster, I am not going to tell the lobster artist how wonderful her drawing is. Even the slowest child knows the difference between a horse and a lobster. Not only will my false praise do nothing to help the child achieve her goal, it will also cause me to lose all credibility with her, and any legitimate praise I may offer later will be meaningless. My job is to help her draw a horse of which she can be justifiably proud. So while developing self-esteem might be high on my list of affective results achieved through art, the way I would accomplish that end is by presenting challenging projects and teaching my students that they can achieve pretty much anything with proper instruction and hard work. If you are a non–art teacher who has been assigned the task of "teaching art," please keep this in mind.

I will now step down from my soapbox and continue roaming the art room. If you were to follow me, you might hear something like the following.

"Janie, I really like the way you are using your pencil lightly, just as we discussed! Make sure all your lines close up to make shapes. Those first shapes you drew will work perfectly! Johnny, I love your composition so far. Remember not to make your shapes too small—you'll have too much trouble filling them in with a crayon. Shelly, that is an outstanding drawing, but it simply isn't going to work for this particular project. Why don't you keep it as a free drawing and try using lighter lines and bigger shapes? Pat, what is the problem with your project? What were the instructions? Tracy, I love your image, but it is so small! We want people to see it! Here's another piece of paper. I want you to do the same picture, only try to make it stretch from here to here. Wow, I love the way this table is working. Kendall, that is going to be wonderful." Essentially, as you can see, I try to find something I can legitimately praise before I offer a suggestion or negative comment, unless I feel the student is not putting forth a sincere effort.

I think a lot also depends on the atmosphere you create in your classroom. From our very first project in first grade, I explain that we are going to be learning how and why artists do what they do, and that means I do my students the courtesy of treating them like serious artists. Serious artists start over a lot and are always trying to improve their work. After I pass out paper, I show students where the extra paper is for those who might need to begin again. It's a given that some people will need to do so, even if it's just because they got a better idea after a few lines. I believe every student can do the project if they try hard enough, and that attitude affects all my actions. I am amazed at the number of adults who have told me about childhood music teachers who told them they couldn't sing. I would never tell a student, "You can't draw." When a student tells me she can't do something, I simply say, "You just haven't done it yet. If I thought everyone already knew how to do this, why would I teach it?" I realize this attitude might be frustrating for students who are struggling and truly feel they can't do something, but part of my job is to help them achieve success in spite of their doubts. Few things feel better than succeeding in an endeavor you thought was impossible or simply making something of which you are truly proud. (One of those "few things" is watching your students do so!)

Having said all this, you will learn over time how far to push a student. I might send a student back two or three times to finish a piece that I feel has too much negative space or needs touch-up in some area, but there will come a time when I know that further effort will be counterproductive. The best outcome is achieved when the student herself recognizes a problem that needs work.

As a result of this constant, ongoing discussion of the students' work, most of my pupils make very good grades. I simply don't accept their projects until I am satisfied that they have done their very best. Hopefully, they will ultimately learn to internalize this process.

First Year

THE **"FIRST YEAR"** described here is the complete curriculum I use in grade one. As discussed in the introduction, this material can easily be condensed and adapted to a higher grade level. Regardless of the target audience, in the first year, I introduce very basic concepts about the elements of art. I also introduce some principles, but as you will see, the units are centered around the elements. I define the elements as color, shape, texture, value, line, and form.

Lesson 1: Creating a Portfolio

Lesson Summary: Students fold 18″ by 24″ tagboard in half and decorate it.

Purpose: To create a portfolio in which to keep artwork.

Materials: 18″ × 24″ 150# white tagboard, 1 piece per student, #2 pencils, markers, colored pencils, and/or crayons

New Vocabulary/Concepts: Portfolio, hamburger fold

Time: One+ period*

Possible Visual Aid: Artist's portfolio

*After Lesson 2, you may decide to have a catch-up period. Pass back both projects and allow students to work on whichever one they want. Whenever you see a "+" sign, it indicates that most students will need more time and that this project will be tied to a project using the same materials for a catch-up period. At the end of the period, I tell my students that we will be doing a different project next time, but they will then have a period to finish both projects.

In every class, the first day of each year is devoted to a discussion of art class rules (see "Getting Started," page 1) and the creation of a portfolio. I am a huge believer in keeping work at school rather than sending it home each day. Obviously, this allows students the opportunity to finish projects they might not otherwise complete. It allows me to see progress and trends I might miss, and I can more easily select work for the spring show. When the portfolio goes home at the end of the year, the parents see a cohesive body of work, not just a series of crumbled papers from a book bag. (Of course, the children can share their works in progress at any time, and I always make sure that parents understand that the children *are* producing and *will* have projects to prove it. I also have student work hanging on the hall walls whenever possible.) Even if you are homeschooling, I strongly recommend keeping work in a portfolio.

I begin the activity by explaining to the students that they are going to keep their work in a portfolio, and I ask them if they know what that is. (Several of my students had portfolios of some sort in kindergarten.) I discuss the fact that the word "portfolio" has two meanings: the actual case or folder in which an artist keeps work (I frequently bring in a professional example), or the work itself. I explain that we will start by making the folder, but by the end of the year, we will have lots of work inside.

Each student is given a piece of 18″ by 24″ 150# tagboard. Because the children are small, I ask them to dangle the tagboard beside their chairs. They should hold it from the top using one hand so that it hangs in a portrait (vertical) position. Then I tell them to grasp the bottom of the tagboard with the other hand, bring the bottom up to the top and press the piece flat on their desks, thus folding it in half, creating a hamburger fold. We briefly discuss the different types of folds I describe in "Getting Started." For older children, it is sufficient to simply show them the type of fold you want. I have them place the resulting 12″ by 18″ portfolio on the desk in front of them in the landscape position with the fold at the bottom. I tell them to raise their left hands and lower them to the bottom left-hand corner of the "page." I have them place their names in pencil in this corner, followed by their grade designation, and then they turn the folder over and do the same thing on the other side. (This way, no matter which side is up in the portfolio cubby, a student will be able to quickly find his or her work.) After they have completed these steps, they may decorate one or both sides of their portfolios in marker, pencil, or crayon.

Lesson 2: Each Artist Is Unique

Lesson Summary: After a brief discussion using visual aids, students will draw a picture that includes at least one tree.

Purpose: Children will understand that each artist is unique, that no two projects should look alike.

Materials: Several posters of artworks that focus on trees, 12″ × 18″ white construction paper, pencils, crayons, markers, and/or colored pencils

New Vocabulary/Concepts: Unique, artists don't copy

Time: One+ period

Possible Visual Aids: Works by Dutch landscape artists like Claude Lorraine or Meindert Hobbema; John Constable; Paul Cornoyer (especially *Plaza After Rain*); Caspar David Friedrich (especially *Tree with Crows*); Henri David Rousseau's jungle scenes; landscapes by Li T'ang and Shen Chou; Currier and Ives; Alfred Sisley; Ernst Ludwig Kirchner's *Forest with Brook*; or any of Piet Mondrian's earlier trees, especially his red trees and apple trees

Before the class begins, select 8 to 10 visual aids depicting trees. The prints should represent a wide variety of styles and cultures. Check the gray box for several suggestions.

Explain to the students that some of the things we study in art class are "what artists do" and "how and why they do them." "Everyone sees the world a little differently, and one thing artists do is to try to share their view of that world—to call our attention to the beauties of nature, the colors around us, the shapes and textures, and so forth. Perhaps they will help us see things in a new or better way." Starting with the most traditional and realistic, show the prints one at a time. Each time, ask the students what the picture depicts and whether the artist did a good job. (You can encourage a positive reply by gently nodding your head as you speak.) If the painting shows more than just trees, point specifically to the trees in the work. When showing each subsequent picture, ask if it looks exactly like the previous one. When the children say no, ask them what is different. Some trees might be bigger or smaller, darker or lighter, leafy or bare, more realistic or stylized. Encourage the children to explore the pictures seriously. After you have completed the series, explain that each artist is unique and that therefore their paintings and drawings, however wonderful, do not look alike. This discussion should take about 10 minutes.

If possible, hang the prints where the children can see them. (I have a magnetic whiteboard, but a stiff print could rest on a chalk trough. There is also a glue that works for temporary adhesion and does not leave marks on the print.) Hold up a sheet of white, 12″ by 18″ construction paper and explain that each of them is going to receive a piece. They may turn their paper in either direction, landscape or portrait (demonstrate). The only requirement for this project is that everyone must start by drawing *at least one tree*. This can be any kind of tree: real or imaginary, evergreen or deciduous, fall, winter, spring, or summer, apple tree, cherry tree, lollipop tree, or cotton ball tree. The important thing is that it be *their* tree—not their neighbor's idea of a tree. Stress this point. While artists may definitely be inspired by other artists, their final work is their own vision. They may use any dry medium for this project: crayon, marker, and/or colored pencil. Once the tree is completed, the student may finish the picture in any way he or she chooses. At the end of the period, you might have the children hold up their pictures so that they can all see what their classmates have done and comment on the fact that (hopefully) in spite of the fact that they all did a terrific job, no two pieces look the same. If some students did not complete their projects, explain that they will have a catch-up period later on.

Lesson 3: Introducing the Elements of Art

Lesson Summary: Students will do rubbings and tracings of leaves.

Purpose: Children will be introduced to the concept of element and the elements of art.

Materials: Thin paper (12″ × 18″ drawing or newsprint paper, or 11″ × 17″ computer paper), crayons, several varieties of leaves, enough for each child, pencil (for name only)

New Vocabulary/Concepts: Element, color, shape, texture, value, line, form, rubbing, tracing

Time: One period

Before the lesson begins, gather a variety of green tree leaves. I try to have three or four kinds. This lesson will work best if the leaves are relatively similar in size (not too huge and not too small) and if at least one variety is very simple in shape. Make sure that they are not too fragile and that the veins stick out strongly on the "underneath" side. Since my class size is usually 20, I gather 20 of each kind. I keep these in a plastic bag, and if they are going to sit for a few days, I place a slightly damp paper towel in the bag. Stack the leaves according to variety and place a stack of each variety on each table, or pass out one of each type to each student.

Explain that the subject of today's lesson is elements of art. If you are dealing with younger children, you will want to explain the nature of an element. Elements are the basic building blocks of our world, and each subject has its own elements. In science, these are the actual elements, such as oxygen, carbon, or hydrogen. I usually explain that water can be broken down into hydrogen and oxygen. Music has elements such as harmony, rhythm, and tempo, while literature has character, plot, or setting. We could break this down further into sentences, words, or letters. Elaborate as much as necessary to get the point across.

Hold up two leaves of approximately the same size but very different species. Make sure the top or darker green side is facing the students. Ask the following questions: "If I am an artist trying to draw a realistic picture of these leaves, what is the most noticeable difference between them? How would you know which is which?" The answer, of course, is their shapes. Shape is an element of art. (Write it on the board.) "How else could I make the leaves look realistic? How would we know they are not fall leaves?" They are green. Green is a color, and color is an element of art. Add it to the list. Point to the stem and veins and ask how you would add them. Elicit the word "line" and add it to the list. Ask the students to pick up a leaf and gently stroke the top and bottom. What is different? Feeling or texture is another element of art. Hold up your two leaves again. Turn one so that the underside is facing out. Ask the students to describe the difference. They are both green, but one is lighter than the other. In art, we call the use of light and dark "value." Draw a simple leaf shape on the board and try to pick it up. Of course you can't, because it has no depth or thickness—it is only a shape. The real leaf, on the other hand has three dimensions, or form, so you *can* pick it up. Form is our sixth element. Explain that the class is going to explore each of these elements throughout the year, but today they are just going to do a project to help them remember all six.

Place a piece of drawing paper or newsprint on the board. Explain that the students are going to do two things with the leaves. Place a leaf on top of the paper and trace it accurately with a crayon. Any color is fine, and the paper may be turned in either direction. After removing the leaf, look at it carefully and draw the veins on the tracing. I usually do only partial examples, because time is an issue. Then place the leaf under the paper in a different spot, vein side up, and do a rubbing of the leaf. (In art, this is technically called "frottage." If you have older students, you might use the term.) Stress good rubbing technique. Don't press too hard or too softly with the crayon, don't leave spaces between crayon lines, don't let the leaf move, and so forth. Tell the students that they must do *at least* one rubbing and one tracing on their paper, but they may do several rubbings and one tracing or vice versa. Leaves may overlap. Older students can be asked to make a more sophisticated composition, or include prints. The results will definitely display color, line, texture, shape, and value, although admittedly form is only implied. If you have great amounts of time, perhaps you could have the students include a cutout that is curled or crumbled. At the end of the class, have the students say the elements again. If possible, save the leaves or gather new ones for students who want to add to the project in a catch-up period.

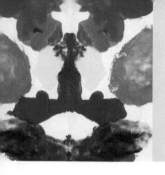

Unit One: **Color**

Our perception of the way light is absorbed, reflected, or refracted

---

If you wish to add an art history component to this unit, you might do so in different ways. You could select a general approach to art in which color is key—like certain types of Expressionism—and discuss how the artists used color to make their points. Or you could accompany the appropriate lessons with examples of different types of colors—primary, secondary, intermediate, and tertiary. Actually, the two approaches might be combined by selecting Expressionist pieces that use different color schemes to show how different colors create different effects.

Lesson 4:   **Magic Colors**

Lesson Summary: Students will mix primary colors to form secondaries (and intermediates).

Purpose: Students will be introduced to the concept of primary and secondary colors.

Materials: 12″ × 18″ white construction paper, tempera paint (preferably magenta, turquoise, and yellow), brushes (size 8 or 9), paper towels, water buckets, pencils (for names only)

Review: Elements of art, color, shape, value, texture, line, and form

New Vocabulary/Concepts: Primary, secondary, two reasons primaries are important (intermediate)

Time: One period

Possible Visual Aid: *Primary Colors* by Kristen Ankiewicz

Before the class begins, place containers of magenta, warm blue (I use turquoise), and yellow tempera paint on the tables. (Red and blue will work, but magenta and turquoise will yield brighter results. The students will still "read" them as red and blue.) Also put out pencils, paper towels, water buckets, and brushes. (Size eight or nine is good, or you can use the brushes that come with watercolor sets.) Ask the students if they remember the six elements of art, and review them. Then ask them if they can guess what element they are going to study today. (Most will guess "color.") Ask them to name the colors on the table. Explain that magenta is a cool red and that turquoise is a warm blue, and use the color names "red, yellow, and blue." Tell them that they are going to do magic, and like all magic, there is a trick to it. Some of them will know the trick, but if they do, they should not tell and ruin the surprise for others.

Start by explaining that our "magic wands" will be our paintbrushes, and that they must be very clean or the magic won't work. Discuss the proper way to clean a paintbrush. First, make sure the bristles reach all the way down in the bucket and stir the brush—don't put the bristles near the top of the water and splash. Then stroke or scrape the wet bristles on the edge of the bucket, don't tap. Finally, dry the bristles on a paper towel, *don't squeeze them with your fingers!* I demonstrate the proper procedure, but I also demonstrate improper methods (with clean water) so that students can see that improper methods can result in spattering water on themselves, their projects, or their neighbor's work. I suggest that any time they work with paints, they should start by cleaning their brushes.

Pass out a piece of white construction paper to each student, and ask them to put their names on the paper with the pencils. They may turn the paper either way. I place a piece of white construction paper on the board. I explain that they are going to do this project along with me, rather than seeing a demonstration. I dip my dry brush fully into the yellow paint and create a fairly thick solid area of paint somewhere on my page, away from the edge. I usually paint a circular shape, but they may make any shape that is about the size of their palms. As soon as this is done, they should clean their brushes. Dip the clean bristles about halfway into the red paint, and say the following magic words: "Abra Cadabra, Abra Cadee! I mix red paint with yellow paint and what do I see?" Stir the red paint into the yellow "splotch" on the paper until the entire area turns orange. Ask if the students got orange "magic." If their paint is too red or too yellow, encourage them to adjust it by adding the appropriate color with a *clean* brush. It is not necessary for all the splotches to look alike, but they should be some sort of orange. Clean the brushes.

Dip your brush fully into the yellow paint again and repeat the first step somewhere else on the page, away from the now orange area. Clean your brush. (The students are following along.) Dip your brush about halfway up into the warm blue (or turquoise) and repeat the magic words: "Abra Cadabra, Abra Cadee! I mix blue paint with yellow paint and what do I see?"

Once again, have the students "stir" the two colors until the entire area turns green, and encourage adjustments. Complete the process by placing an area of magenta (red) on the page and adding a little blue. (You may call the result "violet" or "purple.")

If you look out over the room, you should see that each paper has an area of orange, green, and violet, while the paint containers hold only red, yellow, and blue. Point this out to the students, and ask what a visitor might think. Explain that red, yellow, and blue are magic colors, and ask if anyone knows the other name for them. Usually several children will know the word is "primary." Write it on the board, and ask if anyone knows the two reasons why primary colors are so important. Elicit or explain the following:

"Primary colors are important because you can mix them to make all the other colors, but no other colors can be mixed to make them! That is, if I run out of green paint, I could mix blue and yellow to make more, but if I run out of yellow, I must go to the store and buy more, or borrow some from a friend." (We'll discuss pigments later.) Reinforce this concept. "What could I do if I ran out of orange paint? Blue? Red? Violet?"

Put the primary color names on the board. Ask if anyone knows the name for orange, green, and violet (purple). They are secondary colors. Put that information on the board as well. Ask the students to look at their neighbors' papers. "Are all the oranges the same? The greens? The purples? No. Some greens are yellower and some are bluer. These are called 'intermediates,' and we will discuss them later."

If time allows, let the students mix all three colors to create a rather grayish brown.

Lesson 5: Bernard the Butterfly— Mixing Colors and Symmetry

Lesson Summary: Students will create symmetrical designs using primary colors.

Purpose: The project will reinforce the concept of primary colors, how they create secondary colors, and introduce the concept of symmetry.

Materials: 12″ × 18″ white construction paper, tempera paint (preferably magenta, turquoise, and yellow), brushes (size 8 or 9), paper towels, water buckets, pencils (for names only), a butterfly shape cut from 12″ × 18″ white construction paper

Review: (Within the story) the word "primary," red, yellow, blue, two reasons primary colors are important, orange, green, and violet

New Vocabulary/Concept: Symmetrical

Time: One period

Possible Visual Aids: Photos of colorful real butterflies, Eric Carle illustrations of butterflies and spiders, showing a different interpretation

Before class begins, create the same setup as for "Magic Colors." Fold a piece of 12″ by 18″ white construction paper in half hamburger fold and cut out a symmetrical butterfly. Put aside.

When the students are seated, tell the following story: "Once upon a time, when the world was young, there were no colors! Everything was white—the flowers were white, the sky was white, the grass was white, the animals were white. One day, Mother Nature looked down and said, 'Boring!' So she decided to add color to the world, but she could only carry three buckets of paint. What three colors do you think she took? That's right, red, yellow, and blue. Why did she choose those three? Very good—because she knew she could make all the other colors with them, but no other colors could make them. So there she was, off in a corner painting a garden. She mixed some red and blue to paint the (purple) violets, some red and yellow to paint some (orange) zinnias, and some blue and yellow to paint the (green) grass. She painted the sun yellow and some roses red and the sky blue. And while she was painting, along came a..." (Pick up the paper butterfly, hold it by the centerfold and "flutter" it over to the paint containers. Wait for the children to say "butterfly.") "That's right, a butterfly. This butterfly's name was Bernard. Say 'Hi!' to Bernard." (Bernard says "hi!" back.) "Bernard was a very curious butterfly, and he had never seen anything like this before, so while Mother Nature was busy in the corner of the garden, he got very close and suddenly **SPLAT!**" (Dip a brush into the yellow paint and spatter a good amount of it on one of Bernard's wings. Look very scared. Close the wings and rub.) "Now we know how mothers are—they see everything! So Mother Nature said, 'Bernard, what have you done?'" (Bernard replies in a guilty voice) "'Nothing, I'm just...'" (Mother Nature, in a stern voice) "'Bernard! Show me what you've done!'" (Bernard sheepishly opens his wings, which now display a symmetrical yellow design.) "'Bernard, you know you shouldn't touch things that don't belong to you! But you have given me an idea.' So Mother Nature dipped her very clean brush into the red paint and spattered some on Bernard's wings and had him close and rub them." (Demonstrate.)

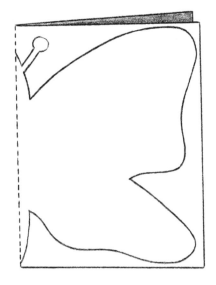

"Then she cleaned her brush and did the same thing with blue." (Demonstrate. Then open and show the final result. Try to create secondaries by overlapping splotches.) "And that's how butterflies got their beautiful colors."

I end by asking if the students think this is a true story. They know it's not, but it's a lot of fun. I also ask what we call designs like butterfly wings that are the same on both sides. In my classes, I usually have students who know the concept of symmetry, but if no one says this, introduce it, write it, and explain.

Give each child a piece of 12″ by 18″ white paper. Have the children fold their piece in half hamburger fold and place their names in pencil on the outside of the folded piece. They should then open the piece and place it "valley" side up on the table. (Their names should not show.) Then they may put paint on one half, fold, and rub. They are to work back and forth between colors, but remind them how important it is to clean their brushes whenever they change colors. Also encourage them to fold and rub often. If they wait too long between rubs, the paint will dry and the resulting design will not be symmetrical. They can always add more of a color. Encourage them to mix colors as well. (If you are working with older children, you can simply focus on the design possibilities and symmetry of this project and forget the story. You might cut butterfly shapes from the finished papers.) Place open projects on a drying rack and clean brushes.

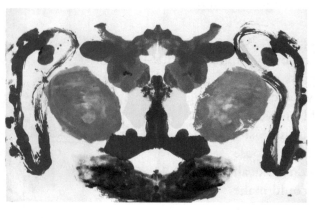

First grader Adam Taylor created this symmetrical design.

Lesson 6: Using a Paintbrush

Lesson Summary: Students will practice a variety of watercolor brush techniques.

Purpose: Students will learn proper ways to use a paintbrush.

Materials: 12″ × 18″ white construction paper, watercolor sets, preferably eight-color with brushes (see discussion under "Materials" in "Getting Started"), paper towels, water buckets, pencils (for names only)

Review: Element of art (color), cleaning brushes

Our next lesson in mixing colors also involves the use of paint, but before we continue, it is necessary to discuss the proper use of a paintbrush. The setup should include water buckets, paper towels, pencils, and enough watercolor sets (brushes included) for each student. Please make sure the paint has decent pigmentation.

Stress to the students that they are going to learn a skill, that today is only for experimentation. The next period, they will be able to paint the most beautiful picture they can, but for this lesson, they are going to focus on the correct way to use a brush. Place a piece of 12″ by 18″ white construction paper on the board, and demonstrate the following techniques. (Make sure you are completely comfortable with them first, of course. Obviously, if you have a more advanced class, you may want to skip this lesson entirely or introduce some more sophisticated methods. You also might have different materials, like tube paints or watercolor paper.)

Rinsing the brush. Review the technique from Lesson 4.

Loading the brush. This is vital. The point of this lesson is primarily to keep the children from "scrubbing" or pressing hard with the brush. Explain that a brush is not like a crayon or pencil. Once the paint is gone, pressing harder won't do any good. Put a little clean water on each color. If the paints are very dry, it might take a little time to get a lot of pigment on the bristles. There should not be puddles in the box, and the students should never "dig" into the paints. Just stroke across the patty until the brush is full of color.

Putting down color. Always pull the stroke in the direction of the handle; use the handle like an arrow. Don't push the brush or stroke sideways. If your bristles look like a bad hair day, you're doing something wrong! Don't go over and over the same area. If your brush is loaded properly, the paint should flow on easily. It shouldn't be sticky-thick or overly watery. Also the ferrule, or metal part, should never touch the paper. Lay down a rich, smooth area of color. The paper should remain smooth. If it looks like suede, you're scrubbing.

Creating a wash. A wash is a very watered-down layer of paint. It is commonly used in watercolor works, especially for large areas like sky. Show two ways to create a wash. One way is to place a coat of clean water on the page and pull a lightly loaded brush through it. The edges of your strokes will be very feathery. Or you may simply water down your pigment until it is very transparent and paint directly on the page.

Create lines of different widths. You should be able to use the very tip of the loaded brush and various amounts of pressure to create lines of different widths.

Printing. Simply load the brush and press it on the page, creating a teardrop shape. Placed in a circle, these prints make great flower petals, or overlapped, they can be animal scales.

After demonstrating these various procedures, pass out paper, ask the students to put their names on the back and then simply practice. They may use any colors, of course, but remind them to clean their brushes well when switching to a new one. Try to discourage painting pictures at this point. Emphasize good technique.

At the end of the lesson, allow a little extra time for cleanup. Caution the children to stroke clean, wet brushes over a paint patty to clean it. Use a clean, dry brush to soak up puddles. The students should not wipe the patties with a paper towel. Check the paint boxes before they are closed.

Lesson 7: Watercolor Painting

Lesson Summary: Students will paint a watercolor picture.

Purpose: Students will practice proper ways to use a paintbrush and review mixing colors.

Materials: 12″ × 18″ white construction paper, watercolor sets (preferably eight-color with brushes), paper towels, water buckets, pencils (for names only)

Review: Element of art (color), primary (red, yellow, and blue), secondary (orange, green, and violet), proper methods of using a paintbrush

Time: One or two periods

Possible Visual Aids: Watercolor paintings by Raoul Dufy or Winslow Homer.

The setup will be the same as Lesson 6. Pass out 12″ by 18″ white construction paper, have the children put their names on the back, and simply let them paint anything they want. You might begin by asking what kinds of colors are in the paint box (primary, secondary, brown, and black). Stress that they may orient their papers in either direction and paint a picture, a design, or a combination of both. But remind them of the techniques they learned in the previous class. They should not press hard with the brush or scrub an area. Encourage them to fill the paper. A painting is not like a drawing, and most paintings are not arrangements of lines or areas of color on a white background. And most importantly, suggest that they mix colors on the paper (not on the patties, of course). They could lay down a wash of blue and place a wash of yellow over it and compare the resulting green to the green right out of the box.

While we will cover the subject at length in a later project, this is a good time to briefly introduce the topic of negative space, the area left over after the artist has finished the subject, or positive space. While there are certainly exceptions, most artists do not leave vast expanses of negative space. I demonstrate the concept by drawing two rectangles on the board about the size of my paper. In one, I line up small, simple flowers (like tulips or daisies) across the bottom, and on the other, I draw the same thing, but I overlap and fill the page with large blooms.

I then ask the students which one they like better. Virtually everyone votes for the better composition. I briefly point out that an artist might paint a small figure on a large background to express loneliness, for example, but we are going to save such approaches for later. I emphasize that it is not what I drew, but how I drew it that made the difference.

Some children will claim to be done rather quickly. If they have left large areas of white, explain that they are not finished until most of the paper is covered. If a student truly does create a nice composition with time to spare, they will probably want to do a second paint-

ing. Place the paintings on a drying rack and clean paint boxes and brushes.

If you are condensing this curriculum for older students, you might want to use this period to create a color wheel instead of free experimentation. (See Third Year, Lesson 2.)

Lesson 8:   Drawing with "Chunk-o-Crayon"

Lesson Summary: Students will draw pictures using red, yellow, and blue Chunk-o-Crayons.

Purpose: Students will learn the concept of intermediate colors.

Materials: Chunk-o-Crayons in primary colors (or large primary-colored crayons with the wrappers removed), 12″ × 18″ white construction paper, pencils (for name only)

Review: Element of art (color), primary, secondary, why primaries are important

New Vocabulary/Concepts: Intermediate, brittle

Time: One+ period (with next lesson)

Possible Visual Aids: The works of Franz Marc, especially *Deer in the Forest I* and *Deer in the Forest II*

Chunk-o-Crayon is a large-format rectangular crayon that is rather pricey, although it lasts for years if it isn't dropped. It comes in primary colors, black, or dappled sticks, 12 to a box. For my purposes, I use the sets of primary colors, although you may have to search the Internet to order these. Each child shares the three hues with the student seated directly opposite, so one box serves eight children. If your budget won't stretch this far, try using old preschool crayons (the large ones) with the wrapper removed. Place the crayons and some pencils on the tables before class. (If you are working with older children, you could skip this lesson and have them incorporate the concepts into their color wheels.)

Ask the children what element of art you have been discussing (color). What colors are on the table? (Primaries or red, yellow, and blue. Elicit both answers.) What do we know about these colors? (They can make all other colors, but you can't make them.) This might also be a great time to discuss the meaning of the terms "primary" (first or basic) and "secondary" (pretty obvious!).

Put a sheet of white paper on the board and color an area somewhat gently using the blue crayon. Color very firmly over this area using the yellow. Create another area using less blue and another using more. Always use the yellow firmly. This should yield a general green, a yellowish green, and a more bluish green. Or start with red and yellow and create orange, yellow-orange, and red-orange. Discuss the fact that when we mix two primaries evenly we get a secondary color, but when we mix them *un*evenly, we get an intermediate. (Depending on the type of pigment being used, this may not be technically true for secondaries, but the concept is easiest to explain this way.) Define the word "intermediate."

Show them that if you use the corner of the crayon, you can make a sharp line, but if you use the side, you can make a broad area of light color. Explain that they may draw anything they want—a picture, a design, or both—but the requirement for this project is to have at least *some* orangey color, some greenish color, and some purplish color. If they can make several different intermediates, that would be great. (They will probably create a variety of hues anyway.) Caution them about filling their entire page with a coat of any one color. I usually demonstrate by filling my whole page quickly with the side of my blue crayon and asking, "If I want to put a bright orange color in this area, will that be possible?" They all realize that pure orange does not contain blue. There will be students who want to simply use the side of their crayons to fill the whole page and end up with swathes of indeterminate hues. Try to encourage them to create secondaries and intermediates first, and save that type of experimentation for the remainder of the picture or their free drawing. Also explain that the Chunk-o-Crayons are brittle (ask what that word means), and ask them not to use them like building blocks or stand them on edge.

Pass out the paper. Their names go on the back in pencil.

Lesson 9: Fall Picture—Creating Tertiaries

Lesson Summary: Children will draw a picture expressing fall using mixed colors.

Purpose: Children will learn the concept of tertiary colors. Children will be encouraged to observe the change of tree colors closely.

Materials: 12″ × 18″ white construction paper, crayons, pencils (for names only)

Review: Element of art (color), primary, secondary, intermediate

Time: One+ period

New Vocabulary/Concept: Tertiary

Possible Visual Aid: Albert Bierstadt, *Autumn* or *Rainy Day in Autumn*

In Indiana, where I teach, this project comes at about the right time of the year. Depending on your location, you might have to adjust it, perhaps using ripening fruit or photos. (Those of you working with older children could skip this lesson and have them incorporate the concepts into their color wheels.)

Ask the students what we call this season. After eliciting "fall" or "autumn," ask what special thing happens outside during this season. Most students will know that leaves change color. "Do the leaves change suddenly? Do you go to bed one night with green trees and wake up the next morning to see orange, red, and yellow? Of course not. They change gradually." At this point, you might explain briefly why the leaves change color—a nice tie-in to science!

Place a sheet of white paper on the board in portrait position. Sketch in a simple trunk with a brown crayon. Use green with a medium pressure to create a large, solid crown. Ask, "What kind of color is green?" (A secondary.) Take an orange crayon and color over one curved side of the crown—fade off about halfway in. Ask, "What kind of color is orange?" (A secondary.) Use some yellow-orange and some red-orange. Make the tree turn progressively more autumnal.

In an area of negative space on the same page, draw a small trunk and use orange to color the crown. Ask the children which one looks more realistic. Explain that sometimes, artists want things to look more realistic and sometimes they want to use color more expressively. Some tree colors are very pure by the end of the fall, but most look a little mixed throughout the season.

Explain that when two secondaries, like orange and green, are mixed together, we call the result a tertiary. I usually digress to discuss the definition of "primary," "secondary," and "tertiary." Tertiaries are unusual colors with unusual names. Before I continue the project, allow me a few moments to climb on my soapbox.

Creating tertiaries in fall trees. (See color insert)

When I was a young art student, there was a distinct difference between the definitions for "intermediate" and "tertiary." An intermediate color is made by mixing uneven amounts of two primary colors. The same result can be achieved by mixing a primary with a related secondary (a secondary next to it on the color wheel; see Third Year, Lesson 2). A tertiary is made by mixing two secondaries. The results are totally different. Now granted, I have not been a young art student for a long time, but the results are still totally different. Intermediates are bright, pure colors, such as red-orange or blue-green. Tertiaries are dull colors with names like olive or bronze (orange plus green), slate (green plus violet), or russet (orange plus violet). (I've heard other terms for the last two.) Many Web sites and other sources now define them interchangeably. They will tell you that the term "tertiary" can refer to a color made by mixing two secondaries or it can be another word for an intermediate.

How is this possible? The results are *totally different!* I urge you to teach the true definitions of these terms. A nice summary of color definitions appears at www.woodfinishsupply.com/ColorTheory.html. Thank you for your kind attention—I will now step down off my soapbox.

I do not care if my students learn the names of the tertiaries. I do give them the term "bronze" for the result of mixing orange and green. I continue by mixing red and yellow with my green to show some other options. Some bushes and trees turn a reddish purple. There are lots of possibilities.

I ask the students to tell me what kinds of things I could put in a picture to let the viewer know it depicts fall. We discuss the trees, leaves falling, piles of leaves, the clothing the children might wear, turkeys and jack-o-lanterns and pumpkins, Halloween costumes, rakes, smoke coming out of chimneys, and so forth. I then tell the children that they may turn their paper either way, their name goes on the back in pencil, and that they need to use crayons. Their picture must start with one tree that uses mixed colors, preferably a tertiary, to create the feeling of fall. After that, they may finish the picture any way they want. They can add more trees, children playing, houses, or whatever they want to make me see "autumn" when I look at it.

Lesson 10: Introducing Complementary Colors

Lesson Summary: The children will view the effects of staring at various colors.

Purpose: Students will learn about complementary colors.

Materials: Black-and-white pictures that yield optical illusions, transparent circles in magenta, cyan, and yellow, a large white surface

Review: Element of art (color), in context of lesson: primary, secondary

New Vocabulary/Concepts: Complementary colors, afterimage, opposite, rods, cones

Time: One period

The following exercise can be used to introduce even the youngest students to the concepts of complementary, or opposite, colors, afterimages, rods, and cones. With minor adjustments, it can be used with any grade level.

You will need some books or reproductions of black-and-white designs that create optical illusions, the kind that vibrate, jump, or wiggle when you stare at them. You might explore the works of Bridget Riley, a famous British Op artist, but there are several books of moiré designs and optical illusions that contain such images. You will also need three fairly large (6″ to 8″) shapes cut from colored acetate, such as overhead projector material or report covers, in magenta (cool red), cyan (warm blue), and yellow as well as a large white background, like a projector screen. If you can create these shapes on a computer and print them on clear overhead projector acetate, you can get the best results. If two of the shapes are overlapped and placed against a white surface, you should be able to easily see a pure secondary.

Introduce the subject of opposites. Ask the children the opposites of several common words. Finish the list with black or white, then ask the opposite of red. Students will make a variety of guesses. Explain that just as black and white are opposites, each color has an opposite of its own, and those opposites behave in very special ways.

Show several examples of the black-and-white designs that vibrate or result in ghost images if stared at. Explain a little about afterimages, how the brain takes little pictures of things we stare at and holds them for a very brief time. Ask them if they have ever "seen" the bright TV screen for a few seconds after they have turned it off. Or perhaps they have retained the image of a lightbulb after it is no longer lit. These are afterimages. It is our ability to retain afterimages that allows us to watch movies and cartoons. If our brain did not retain a brief visual memory of each movie frame as the film went by, we would see a pretty jerky show.

Just like a real camera, our brain takes these pictures as negatives—that is, the lights are dark, the darks are light, and each color is retained as its opposite. If your students have never seen photographic negatives, it might be nice to have some handy. Or, if your room is technologically equipped, you might use a program like PhotoShop to invert a color picture so that they get the idea.

Explain that our eyes have receptor cells called rods and cones. Rods receive sensations of light and dark, and cones receive sensations of color. We can overwork these cells. Have you ever come into a normally lit building from extremely bright sunlight? Or entered a darkened movie theater from a well-lit lobby? It can take your rods a few seconds to adjust. Some people think this may account for the blinking effect you get when you stare at black-and-white patterns. Others think it has something to do with confusing your brain about which is the background—the black or the white. Whatever the answer, we can use these facts—that the brain holds a brief impression of an image, and the impression is a negative, or opposite, of the original—to find the opposite of any color we want.

Using a projector screen or other large white background, hold one of the acetate shapes firmly against it. I usually start with magenta. Ask the children to stare at the shape for about 30 seconds. They may blink occasionally, but it is important for them to keep their eyes focused on the center of the shape. Explain that when the 30 seconds are over, you are going to pull the shape away and that they must keep their eyes focused on the white background until the afterimage forms. This may take a couple of seconds, but you will know when they see it, because their faces will simply light up. Ask them what color they see. If you hold up a magenta (a cool or pinkish red) shape, the afterimage should appear to be green. (If a student doesn't see anything, it is probably because he or she let their eyes wander at some point, but it could imply a color perception problem. You might want to have a book with the designs used to test color blindness handy. These can be obtained at the library.)

Ask the class to tell you the opposite of red. They will now say green. Ask them the opposite of green. Most will realize that it works both ways, but it is a good idea to reinforce the concept with a demonstration. (Besides, kids can't get enough of this exercise.) Hold up all three shapes. By the time you reach this project, your students will already be familiar with how the primary colors mix to form secondaries. Hold the magenta in one hand and the other two primaries in the other. Explain that even though you don't have a green shape to stare at, you do have a blue and a yellow. Place one over the other to make a green shape. It is important that all your shapes be identical so that there is no edge of another color showing.

Repeat the process that you used for staring at the magenta shape. When you pull the "green" shape away, the children should see a magenta afterimage. You can then do the same exercise using the blue acetate, which should result in an orange afterimage. Since you have no orange acetate, you will once again have to make it by mixing the other two primaries. Finally, hold up the yellow shape and stare. The violet afterimage is my favorite, which is why I save it for last. Make purple by overlapping the magenta and the blue and prove the converse by staring. By now, many of my students are able to predict that the opposite of yellow will be purple, either because it is the only secondary left, or because they have reasoned out that the opposite of each primary color is the secondary color you get when you mix the other two primaries.

If you have a color wheel in your room, now is a great time to point out that opposite colors lie directly across from—or opposite—each other on the color wheel. Explain that every color has an opposite, and that if it is a color wheel color—not brown or ochre or a tertiary—it will lie directly across from its opposite on the wheel. Artists call opposite colors complementary. I like to point out the difference between a "complement" and a "compliment" and to discuss the root of the word "complete." Any two complementary colors actually contain all three primaries in some proportion, so in a sense you have a complete color wheel. You should also remind the children that because pigment and light have different primaries, the complements will be different as well.

Lesson 11: Red Grass and Orange Sky— An Opposites Picture

Lesson Summary: Students will draw a picture using the opposite of the "normal" colors.

Purpose: This lesson will reinforce the student's knowledge of complementary colors.

Materials: 9″ x 12″ white paper, markers, pencils

Review: The element of art (color), in context of lesson: complementary, red/green, blue/orange, yellow/violet

Time: Two periods

Once your students are familiar with the three basic pairs of opposites, you can do an enjoyable hands-on project to reinforce the concept. You will need white paper (approximately 9″ by 12″), pencils, and markers. If you do not have markers, use crayons very solidly and brightly.

Choose subjects that have a specific color. That is, if I say sky, the first color that pops into your head is probably blue. As I explain to my students, artists can make the sky any color they want, and we all know that the real sky is not always blue, but for this project only we are going to use the most common color we can think of for the subject. In first grade, I use the following: sky (blue), sun (yellow), cloud (white), brick house (red), grass (green), mountains (purple), roof (black), and an orange tree (green crown, orange oranges, brown trunk). I have also used fruits, but I have found that this house—tree—mountain image works best. You could adapt this in several ways for older students. You could certainly allow them to select their own subjects (provided they have a strong color association). It would also be a fun project to do on a computer.

Have each child fold a 9″ by 12″ piece of paper in half hamburger style to create two 6″ by 9″ areas, and place his or her name on the outside. Open the piece and place it valley (blank) side up. On one side of the fold only have them draw the picture lightly in pencil. Leave the other half blank. In this project, I do an example on my whiteboard, explaining that for this picture, creativity is not the main point, so that just this once, their projects may look something like mine. Try to make sure the tree, house, cloud, and so on are not too tiny. They may embellish the house with a door and window. The oranges on the tree are just circles. Everything should be kept simple and they should try not to cross the fold line.

Now for the fun part. You will explain that they are going to color each part of the picture in the opposite color of the one they would normally use. Ask what color they usually think of when someone says sky. They will all say blue. Write "sky" on the board and ask the children the opposite of blue. When they respond with the correct color, write "orange" next to "sky." Since I have a whiteboard, I actually use an orange marker to do this. Proceed to the next item. Go through the entire list and write the opposite color next to each word in a place that can remain in view for reference as long as the children are doing the project. When you get to the tree trunk, explain that every different brown has its own opposite, but that they are going to treat this brown as a dark orange. Ask them the opposite of "dark" and "orange." If you have pastel markers in your room, you can offer them light blue for the trunk. If not, use a warm blue crayon (like robin's egg or azure) or a green-blue crayon, and color lightly.

I actually create a large colored example on the whiteboard next to the list. It is very easy for a student to forget the point and color things their "normal" colors.

Explain to the students that they are going to draw their outlines lightly with pencil first. (This will allow you to make sure they are not missing anything, that items are not too small, and so forth.) They will then use markers to complete their projects, and it is important to color as neatly and solidly as possible. Be sure they fill the entire sky with orange, not just a stripe across the top of the page. Ask them if they can guess why they are leaving one half of their paper blank. They will make a variety of guesses, and someone may actually get the idea: that after they finish coloring the picture in its "opposite" colors, they are going to stare at the center of the colored half for 30 seconds and then at the white half until the afterimage forms. In the afterimage, of course, the sky will be blue, the grass green, the sun yellow. If no one guesses correctly, you can provide some subtle clues.

When a student finishes coloring, have him or her hold the project at arm's length and count slowly to 30. It is important to hold the picture still, so have them rest their entire arm on the desk. If they do not get a clear afterimage, have them focus on a small part of the picture at a time.

If you are working with small children, you might bring in a copy of *Hello, Red Fox*, by Eric Carle, which is about complementary colors.

Lesson 12:   Cut-Paper Complementary Color Project

Lesson Summary: Students will glue cut-paper snowflakes onto opposite colored backgrounds.

Purpose: The project will reinforce the concept of complementary colors and demonstrate the phenomenon of simultaneous contrast.

Materials: 12″ × 6″ and 12″ × 18″ pieces of construction paper in red, yellow, warm blue, orange, green, and violet, scissors, pencils (for names only), glue sticks

Review: Element of art (color), complementary, pairs (red/green, blue/orange, yellow/violet)

New Vocabulary/Concepts: Simultaneous contrast, when placed next to each other opposite colors intensify each other, when mixed opposite colors dull each other

Time: Three periods

Possible Visual Aids: Winslow Homer, *Snap the Whip*; certain pieces by Victor Vasarely

You will need six different colors of 12″ by 18″ construction paper: your brightest red, warm blue or turquoise, yellow, violet, orange, and green. Cut some of the pieces into 12″ by 6″ sections and have enough for each child to have one section of each color, with a few extras for mistakes. You will also need scissors, pencils, and glue sticks.

"For artists, it is very important to know the opposite of each color and to understand how complementary colors behave. When complementary colors are placed next to each other, they make each other seem much brighter. They can almost glow, or they can cause the vibration effect we saw in the black-and-white patterns we started with.

"When you stared at the colored shapes, you probably noticed that long before I pulled the shape away, a 'halo' of the opposite color formed around the shape. Every color we look at is accompanied by a halo of its opposite, but we don't usually notice it. This halo has an effect upon the color next to it, however, and this effect is known as 'simultaneous contrast.' In the case of complements, the halo serves to brighten the neighboring color. If I place a red shape next to a green shape, the red shape will 'cast' a green light all around itself. Where the green halo falls on the green shape, it will have the effect of increasing the amount of green light that is hitting my eye. The same will be true of the green shape's red halo as it crosses the red shape."

You can demonstrate this effect very easily by holding a piece of red construction paper right next to a piece of green. Ask the children to stare at the line where the two overlap and they will see the line start to vibrate, or they might even see it turn white or black. Artists use this effect in a variety of ways, from grabbing our attention in an ad to designing fabrics and wallpapers.

When complementary colors are mixed, on the other hand, they dull each other. *True opposites are the only pairs of colors you can mix without getting a new color.* If you mix true opposites equally, you should get gray or black. (I stress the concept of true opposites, because the materials that we are given in school are rarely "true" colors. The orange crayon or paint may be a great color, but it is usually not the orange that is the opposite of the blue in the same set. So if you try to demonstrate the dulling properties of opposites, you need to play around with turquoises and magentas and such or you will get a sort of nasty brownish tone rather than a gray.) Reds and greens work best. If you mix true complements unequally, you will get a grayer version of the color you have more of. That is, if I add a few drops of red paint to a cup of green, I should get a duller green, not a bluer green or a yellower green. It will be a different intensity (brightness) of green, and perhaps (but not necessarily) a different value, but not a different hue. At this point in the discussion, simply put a good amount of green tempera on a piece of white paper and add a very small amount of red to it. You might want to thin the result with water to show the dullness a little better. Add more and more red until the result looks black.

Obviously, an understanding of such color theory is vital to artists in several fields. The Impressionists, for instance, painted under the theory that the color of the shadow cast by an object was the complement of the object's color, a concept first suggested by Leonardo da Vinci. I usually ask the following questions: "Let's pretend I'm painting a bowl of fruit, and I want my red apples to look bright and luscious, but no matter how much red paint I add, they just don't seem as bright as I want them. What can I do? That's right, I can put some green next to them. I could put them in a green bowl or against a green background. Now let's say I am painting a bowl of fruit and all anyone can see are my red apples. They are much brighter than the bananas or grapes or pears. I don't want to change their color. I want them to be red apples, not green. What can I do? Very good! I can put a little bit of green in my red paint to tone down the red without changing the color."

In this project, we are going to focus on the ability of opposites to intensify each other. Many of the children will probably have had experience cutting snowflakes, but a short demonstration is a good idea. Pick up one of the pieces of 6″ by 12″ colored paper. Fold it in half hamburger fold and then again, either hamburger or taco. Explain they must have at least two folds, but they may fold it in half once more if they choose. They may cut off corners, but not a complete side. Any shapes they cut out should be fairly large, and they must cut a whole shape out, not just a slit. You want plenty of paper cut away. A good suggestion is that the amount of paper cut away should be as great as the amount left.

Open up the cut paper and view the lacy results. Let's say you used orange. Ask what the opposite of orange is, and when the students say "blue," pick up a 6″ by 12″ piece of blue paper. Place a thin layer of glue on the back of the orange snowflake and stick it on the blue paper, centering it so that the edges meet all around. Why can't they put the glue on the blue background? Of course, the glue will show through the holes! Once the piece is glued, the child is to turn it over and put his or her name on the back.

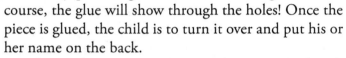

The students are going to make one set of each complementary color pair. They can start with any color, but once they have a set that is orange on blue *or* blue on orange, they are done with those colors. (This project, including the introduction, usually takes more than one half-hour period. If a student must put a name on a snowflake to identify it for the next class, make sure the glue goes on the side with the name when it is glued to the background.)

When a pupil has all three sets completed, explain the next step. The children are going to glue the three pieces onto a 12″ by 18″ piece of paper. This should be the same color as one of the backgrounds, although theoretically, none of it will show. There are two formats the students can use to arrange the pieces on the page and within those formats, they can put them in any order. When the pieces are glued down, be sure the child puts his or her name on the back of the project.

If you are working with older students, you can adapt this project or change it entirely. For instance, you might ask the students to paint or color a picture or design in which the same exact color appears to be different at different places in the composition.

Lesson 13:   File and Free

Lesson Summary: Students may use the period to work on unfinished pieces or create free drawings.

Purpose: Students will have extra time to work on unfinished pieces, or they may have an opportunity to create freely, unconstrained by project requirements.

Materials: Paper (I usually offer 12″ × 18″ and 9″ × 12″ white, and children can ask for colors if they want), materials in the baskets

Review: You might begin with a final review of all the color vocabulary learned thus far.

Time: One period

At the end of each unit, I try to include a period I call "file and free." While I have other catch-up periods throughout the unit, there are usually still several students who can use the time productively. I simply pass out all unfiled work and the portfolios. Depending on your approach and the age of the children, you might insist that students use the time to complete unfinished projects, or you may give them the option of using the time for free drawing. I admit that I'm pretty loose with young children, but as we get closer to the spring show, I do try to encourage slower students to use this time to finish better pieces. At the end of the period, all class projects will be filed. Students may take home free drawings or file them as well.

Unit Two: **Value**

How the artist uses light and dark

While value is a quality of color, it can also exist separately, and many artists use value without color. Your visual aids and/or art history component could focus on works by an artist like Kathe Kollowitz, a continuation of the Expressionist approach from Unit One, or on a completely different genre, such as Chinese or Japanese landscape paintings that use only black ink on silk.

Lesson 14: **Introducing Value**

Lesson Summary: The teacher will use various demonstrations and discussion to explore why we see color and the nature of black and white.

Purpose: Children will be introduced to the physics of light and the definition of "value."

Materials: A room (such as a closet) that can be totally darkened, a prism or "prismatic" glasses, something white, something black

New Vocabulary/Concepts: Physics of light, value, why we see color, black and white are not colors

Time: One period

At Sycamore, I introduce my students to the science of light in the first grade. With some modifications, the following techniques could be adapted to older students who have never studied this area. You will need access to an interior, windowless storage room or closet that will hold several people. You will also need a prism or similar device. I prefer the plastic glasses that act like a prism by fracturing light into spectra when you look through them. These can be bought at certain stores and museums, and sometimes from catalogs.

Ask the children to look around the room and tell you where the color is. Most will point to the pictures on the walls, bulletin boards, clothing, construction paper—whatever they see that seems colorful to them. Some will say that the color is everywhere. Take them into the room with no windows and shut the door. Ask them to look at all the colors in the room. Since I use an art storeroom, this is easy; however, even in a rather dull janitor's closet they will find some colors, and they will always have their own clothing, if nothing else. Turn the light off briefly. Have them describe what they see and try to elicit the word "black" as well as "dark." Ask them where the color went, and repeat the lights-out if necessary until they get the point. Return to the art room and once again ask the children where the color is. Most will realize by now that the color is in the light. Since the color is in the light, and black is what you get when you take away the light, then you have also shown that black is not a color, it is the absence of light.

Once you have shown that you must have light in order to have color in general, you are ready to discuss the reason we see individual colors. Explain that the light we get from our sun is called white light and that it contains all of the colors in the rainbow mixed together. Set up your prism or hand out the plastic glasses and show the children the phenomenon of rainbows created when white light is passed through something that breaks it into its component parts. I explain that different colors of light have different wavelengths and speeds, so each one passes through the material differently. This is also a great time to discuss why we sometimes see rainbows in the sky. When all the colors of light mix together, they result in a perfectly clear light that we call white. (We will explain why we call it "white" in a few minutes.)

Some of you may be familiar with the spinning tops that come with interchangeable disks of various colors. These are frequently sold in children's museum shops or science stores, and I'm sure they are available in many different catalogs. When you spin certain colors fast enough, they will create white, which is another nice demonstration to include in this presentation.

So far, we have proven two points: the color is in the light, and the light can be divided into different colors. At the point in the year that I introduce this unit, the children have already had several sessions with paints of various sorts, so I can ask them, "When all the colors in your paint box are mixed together, do they make white?" Even if a student has just joined the class, they have probably worked with easel paints in kindergarten or preschool, so they know that when they mix all their paints, they get a brownish-gray mush. If your students have not worked with a colored medium, you might do a demonstration in the front of the room or have each child mix crayon or chalk or paint colors at their seats. They will quickly see that when pigments are blended together, they do not make white or clear. Since we have already discussed primary colors by this time, I also explain that the primary colors of light are red, green, and blue rather than red, yellow, and blue. (Primary colors of light are important for the same two reasons: they can be mixed to create all the other colors, yet no other colors can be mixed to form a primary.)

So, pigments are different than light. Pigment is a substance that causes light to be absorbed or reflected in ways that result in the appearance of color. At this point I find a student who is wearing a pure color, like red. I stand behind the child and ask the class why the shirt, or sweater, or whatever, looks red. Even gifted first graders have usually not covered this yet. So I explain it in the following way.

"Janey's shirt is having a party, and all the colors want to come, but in order to get in, they have to be invited in. All the colors of the rainbow are in the white light that is hitting the shirt. The yellow light knocks on the shirt" (here I "knock" on the child's shoulder) "and asks, 'Can I come in?' The shirt says, 'Sure! You are very welcome!' Then the green light knocks. 'Can I come to the party?' 'Sure, come right on in!'" I repeat this for orange, blue, and violet. "Then the red light knocks on the shirt and asks, 'Can I come to the party?' And the shirt says, 'No! We are completely full, and there is no room for any more light.' For some reason, the pigment in this shirt will not allow red light in. The red light has to go somewhere, so it bounces off the shirt and hits my eye. The sensation travels up my optic nerve to my brain. If you were born in the United States, you probably learned to call this sensation 'red.' What would you call it if you were born in Spain?" (Since our students all study Spanish, they know the answer to this question is "rojo.") "Does anyone know what you would call this sensation in France? What about China?" Obviously, the greater the ethnic mix in your class, the more color words you can elicit.

I used to explain this process in a slightly different way, but several years ago a first grader suggested the party scenario, and the other students just loved the image. Obviously you could come up with many others—magic keys or special doorways or passwords, for example. I find that when we review this entire concept in second grade, the "party" image has really stuck!

There are several nice lessons that can be introduced on the concept of pigment. You might discuss the pigment "chlorophyll," which won't let green light in, and how it leaves some trees in the fall, allowing us to see the true colors of the trees. Or you could discuss melanin, the pigment in skin, and why two people can have very different skin tones even though we all share the same pigmentation. What about protective coloration?

After the single color explanation, I find something in the room that is black and I ask the children who is coming to this party. (If a student guesses that the black light could not get in, I ask if there is black in a rainbow.) Most students will guess "all of the light" or "none." Remind the children of their experience in the dark room. What caused the sensation of black? It occurred when no light hit their eyes. If no light is bouncing off to hit their eyes, then all the colors must be at the party. There are two reasons why the eye might perceive black. Either there is no light source at all, such as in the dark room, or all (or most) of the light is being absorbed by an object.

Turn to something in the room that is white or hold up a piece of paper and ask who is attending this party. When normal light hits an object and none of it is allowed in, it all bounces back and hits our eye at once. When all the light mixed together bounces off something, we perceive that object as white. If such light simply hits our eye without bouncing off of something, it appears to be clear. We will discuss more about white light later.

For artists, black and white are not colors. They are *values*. "Value" refers to how the artist uses light and dark. White is the lightest light and black is the darkest dark, although now that artists are using actual light in installations and conceptual pieces, it is possible to have intense wattage that might be considered lighter than white. Each color has value, and there are also a huge variety of grays. This might be a great place to relate light to heat. We usually discuss why white clothing is cooler than black clothing, or why you might choose different values for roofs in different climates.

Lesson 15: Black Crayon on White Paper

Lesson Summary: The students will draw a picture or design using black crayon on white paper.

Purpose: Children will learn the concept of gradation and practice creating it.

Materials: 12″ × 18″ white construction paper, black crayons, pencils (for names only)

Review: Value, black, white, why we see color

New Vocabulary/Concept: Gradation

Time: One+ period (with Lesson 16)

Possible Visual Aids: Sumi brush paintings; sketches by Leonardo da Vinci or Michaelangelo

Begin with a review of the concepts learned in the previous class. It might go something like this: "Where is the color in this room? Very good—in the light. So what element of art did we introduce last time? That's right, value.

Who can define value?" (Avoid the response "black and white.") "Remember, I want a definition, not an example. A definition is always true and explains the idea to someone from another planet. Black is a value and white is a value, but the definition of 'value' itself is—right!—light and dark. Think about color. If I asked the definition of color and someone said 'red,' that would be a great example, but it's not the whole concept of color—it's not a definition. That would be something like 'the effect of light bouncing off of something and hitting our eye.' So value refers to how an artist uses light and dark. What's the lightest light there is? Right: white. And the darkest dark? Great, black!" (Write "black" and "white" on the board. Leave a large space between them.) "There are different ways we can go from the darkest dark to the lightest light. We could start with a very light color like yellow and get progressively darker, like going around a color wheel. We could start with a cup of red paint in the middle and add more and more white paint to it until we reached almost white. We could take another cup of red paint and add more and more black until we reached almost black. We'll talk about these methods later. If I wanted to go from white to black through other values *without using color,* what would I call those middle values?" (Elicit the term "gray.") Place a piece of white paper on the board, and using a black crayon, color heavily to create a rich black area. Decrease the pressure gradually as you move along to create a "shaded" strip.

Explain that when a value goes slowly from dark to light, we call this "gradation." Put some shapes on the board that go gradually from small to large. Emphasize the term "gradually" and show its relationship to "gradation." Put these words on the board and ask the children for other words with the root "grad." Elicit and define words such as "graduate," "graduation," and "grade." Explain that artists must be able to use gradation to create shading on such figures as spheres. Value may go suddenly from dark to light (demonstrate), which we call contrast, or gradually, as in gradation.

Once you have explained grays and gradation, this is essentially a free drawing. The students will use white paper (the lightest light) and a black crayon (the darkest dark). The students may turn their paper either way and draw any kind of picture or design, as long as they create as many values as possible. Remind them that white is a value, so they can't cover the entire page with a gray. Ask them to create gradation somewhere on the page. Names go on the back in pencil. (For older students, you might use charcoal or conte crayon and introduce shading.)

There is one other concept you might use effectively in this lesson plan. Observational drawing is an extremely important aspect of a child's art experience. You might put objects on the tables and have the students render them instead of just drawing from their imaginations. I have used plants and ship models and even other pupils, but you could allow the children to explore the room to find a subject that interests them.

First grader Josh Parquet used gradation and contrast in this lively drawing.

Lesson 16: Using Black and White on Colored Paper—Introducing Tint and Shade

Lesson Summary: Students will draw a picture on colored paper using black crayon and white chalk (or a variation of this lesson).

Purpose: Students will practice creating gradation of value and learn the concepts tint and shade.

Materials: 12″ × 18″ construction paper in various colors, including the primaries and secondaries

Review: Value, black, white, gradation

New Vocabulary/Concepts: Tint, shade

Time: One+ period

Possible Visual Aids: Certain works by Josef Albers; Albrecht Durer, *Praying Hands;* virtually any realistic still life or the artists mentioned

There are several ways to approach this project, depending on the age of the student and the time available. I have chosen the simplest materials— construction paper in various colors, black crayon, and white chalk—since time is a factor in my curriculum. I will suggest an alternative at the end of the lesson.

Begin the class with a review of the concepts you have covered so far, including the element of art (value), its definition (light and dark), where the color is (in the light), the darkest dark (black), the lightest light (white), how we can go from dark to light without using color (grays), and gradation. Explain that, as we discussed previously, we can go from dark to light using color as well. Put up a piece of colored construction paper. Red works well for this demonstration. With your black crayon, make a rich black area and then create gradation so that more and more of the red paper shows through. From even a relatively short distance, this should create the illusion of various dark values of red. Explain that when we add black to a color, we don't change the color itself, only its value. "Why can we add black to a color without changing the color? Right! Because black is not a color. Could I darken red by adding purple? No, I would get red-violet, not a darker red. A color with black added is called a shade." (Write "shade" on the board.) "Where do we find shade outside? Where the light is reduced, as under a tree or where a building blocks the sun. What words have the same root as 'shade'?" (Try to elicit words like "shadow" and "shading.") "Does anyone know the name for a dark value of red?" (The answer is "maroon.")

Using white chalk, create as light an area as possible on the red paper, then use gradation the way you did with the black crayon. The result should be various lighter values of red. (It is better to use chalk than crayon because the pigment in most white crayons is inadequate to cover the area solidly.) Ask the students to describe the result. Someone will probably say "pink." Pink is a tint of red. A "tint" is a color with white added. (Write "tint" on the board.)

We tend to use the term "shade" very loosely. We say things like "That's a lovely shade of pink," even though pink is a tint, not a shade; but that's fine, because the word can mean a subtle variety. Sometimes we're picky and sometimes we're not.

If time allows, you might look for students dressed in different values of the same color, perhaps a variety of denim blues, and ask the children to arrange them from dark to light.

Allow the students to choose their favorite from a variety of basic colors of 12″ by 18″ construction paper. After putting their names on the back in pencil, they may draw anything they want using black crayons and white chalk, but the picture or design should have as many different values of the color as possible, from the deepest shade to the lightest tint. Remind everyone that the true color of the paper is a value as well, so they shouldn't cover the entire sheet with crayon and chalk. They may turn the paper either way.

I usually have a combined catch-up period for this project and the previous one before moving on.

If you have time, you might use other approaches to this project. Obviously this is another great opportunity for observational drawing, and using dark and light on a medium value ground is a time-honored approach to sketching. Look at drawings by such artists as Honore Daumier, Peter Paul Rubens, Jean Auguste Ingres, or Edgar Degas, and encourage older children to try this approach. Another possibility is to give each student tempera paints in black, white, and a primary or secondary color of their choice. Using the pure color they have selected, they should paint a meandering line about an inch wide from one end of a piece of 12″ by 18″ white construction paper to the opposite edge. On one side of the line, they should paint lines of greater and greater value by adding more and more white. On the other, they should decrease the value of the lines by adding more and more black. If there are negative spaces left over, you could treat them in different ways, adding pure values or the pure color. Or cut them out when the piece is dry and mount the page on a piece of construction paper in the complementary color—whatever looks nice. For a similar approach, paint the central stripe with rich watercolor in a primary or secondary color. For the darker values, add black watercolor, and for the lighter values, add more water. Or you might use the tempera or watercolor to create shapes about two or three inches across and surround some with gradations of tint and some with gradations of shade. When the value rings meet, the student could decide what to do.

Lesson 17: Watercolor Fingerprints— Value as a Property of Color

Lesson Summary: Students will create a picture or design using watercolor fingerprints.

Purpose: Children will explore the different values of various colors, as well as reviewing gradation.

Materials: 12″ × 18″ white construction paper, watercolor paint sets with brushes removed, water buckets, paper towels, pencils (for names only)

Review: Value (definition), black, white, gray, tint, shade, gradation

New Vocabulary/Concept: Every color has value

Time: One or two periods

Possible Visual Aid: Any work of art with multiple colors

The setup for this lesson is similar to the earlier watercolor projects, but I suggest you remove the brushes from the paint sets.

Begin the period with a review of value-related concepts. Aside from the element we are studying, the definition of value, tint, shade, black, white, gradation, and gray, review the two ways you have discussed to go from the darkest dark to the lightest light (through grays without color and through tints and shades of a single color). The third way an artist can go from dark to light is through different colors. Some colors are darker or lighter than others. If I open a box of crayons, my yellow crayon is obviously lighter than my purple. I can make the purple lighter by adding white, but in its pure state, it is simply darker than the yellow.

Place a piece of white construction paper on the board. Dip one finger in water and rub the pad of it around on a patty of paint in the watercolor box. I usually use black for this first demonstration. When your finger is loaded with a rich amount of the color, press it on the paper, lift, and press it again next to the first imprint. Continue lifting and pressing in a line without reloading the paint until your finger is dry. Sometimes you might need to rock your finger from side to side to get the paint off. This should create gradation. Show how effective this technique can be. Clean your finger and, using green, create the crown of a tree, overlapping your fingerprints slightly and filling the shape randomly. Only get more paint on your finger when it is totally dry. The effect should be very haphazard and textural. Using brown paint, create a trunk on the tree. I usually create a red brick house with a black shingle roof. Using my finger horizontally, I place the fingerprints in very organized rows to make the bricks. I use my finger vertically to make the shingles, but the values for both should still be very random. Create a flower or sun using yellow or orange or a combination.

(See color insert)

You might suggest that this would be a super approach to flowers or scales or dinosaur hide. Point out the effect of the various values of color versus the gradation of single colors.

Explain to the students that they are going to create a picture using this technique. Remind them to use only the pads of their fingers—their nails should never touch the paint. They may use different fingers, but only two or three should be dirty at the end of the project. Also remind them that they should only get more paint when their finger is totally dry, and that they should not slide or drag their finger, but lift and print. They may do a picture or design and orient their page in either direction, but they should try to use as many different paints from their boxes as possible. Give each student a piece of 12″ by 18″ white construction paper and have them put their name on the back in pencil. These projects should not ever be particularly wet, but it is still a good idea to use a drying rack.

Lesson 18: Value Collage

Lesson Summary: Children will create a collage using materials that have no color.

Purpose: Children will see how contrast affects visibility, and the project will reinforce the concept of value as an element.

Materials: Various colorless materials, such as duct tape, electrical tape, white straws, gray, black, or white fabric, etc., glue sticks, 12″ × 18″ construction paper in white, black, and gray(s), pencils (for names only)

Review: Value (definition), black, white, gray, as property of color, etc.

New Vocabulary/Concepts: Contrast, collage

Time: Two periods

Possible Visual Aids: Collages by Pablo Picasso or Romare Bearden

In this final value project, you will not be using any color. Value is an interesting element, because we can discuss it at length as a property of color. In the second-year curriculum, you will study it extensively in that context, and you have already explored that aspect of value in the previous lessons. But value is a separate element because it can also stand alone, and you want to reinforce this concept before you move on.

For this project, you will need a large collection of various colorless materials. I use black electrical tape, white plastic tape (available from catalogues), black and/or white masking tape (and gray, if you can find it), duct tape, tin foil, white straws, and other materials as I find them. These might be rolls of textured shelf cover in white or black rubberized materials, interesting cloth, strips of lace edging, paper doilies, and even newspaper pages. Divide the materials into equal groups so that each table or station has the same selection. You will also need 12″ by 18″ construction paper in (preferably) black, white, and at least one gray. I offer two grays, one dark and one light, but if cost is a factor, you could do the project with only white or black. Add glue sticks, scissors, and pencils and you are ready to begin.

Place the materials (except for the construction paper) on each table before the children enter. After they are seated, ask them what is the same about all the materials. Be sure they understand you are not talking about the glue sticks or pencils or any tape cores, but the actual materials themselves. This far into the unit, most of the students should recognize that these items have no color, only value. Review the definition and basics of value. Explain that they are going to use these materials to create a project, and ask if anyone knows what a collage is. If you have children who don't, explain that a collage is a work of art in which different types of materials are attached to a background. Put the word on the board, discuss the difference between the word "college" and "collage" and explain that the latter word is French. I suggest that one way to remember the word is to think about a "*coll*ection" of different things making a "*coll*age." If someone makes a project by overlapping only paper, like photos, we call that a montage.

Explain that each student will get to choose from different values of construction paper for the background. Hold some white tape or lace against a piece of white paper and ask if anyone can see it easily. It is perfectly fine to use such combinations—in fact, shiny black tape can be very interesting against the dull black paper—but they should think carefully about their choices. If they want something to be easily seen, they should use a lot of contrast. Put the word on the board and explain that "contrast" is the word artists use to mean "difference." The more difference there is between something and its neighbor, the more it stands out and the more quickly we see it. Since I have a whiteboard, I write the word "contrast" with yellow marker and with black and ask which is more visible. Or I might ask, "If a green frog wants to hide from a predator, does it want to sit in the grass or on a red rock?" Explain that they will also want to think about balancing their values. It rarely works to put all the darks on one side and the lights on the other. Finally, discuss the fact that this is a collage, not a sculpture as such. While the materials will stick out a little, this project must ultimately fit in their portfolio. (Of course, you may have reasons to modify this lesson and make it into a sculpture, but for my purposes, sculpture comes later.)

I caution them about sharing the materials. If all that is left of a piece of cloth is a remnant the size of their background, they may not use the whole thing. They should cut some but leave plenty for others. Since I use a lot of tapes, I discuss the fact that these need no glue, and in fact, they can be used to affix other materials, especially the straws. The duct tape can be difficult to cut, so I demonstrate some strategies, such as letting the roll hang down and using the neck rather than the tip of the scissors. I also remind them that the glue only goes on the back of the piece they are gluing, not on the big paper.

There is one other situation you might discuss. Occasionally, I have a student who makes a wonderful composition and then covers the whole thing with a piece of cloth or tin foil. Suggest that if they want to use a large piece of tin foil, they might consider putting that down first and placing the other materials on top.

Allow each child to choose one of the values of construction paper as the background. The paper may be turned in either direction, but for this project we place our names on the front in pencil. Stress the concept that this should be out of the way in a corner where it does not interfere with the composition. If a student cuts out a nonsticky material right before clean up, they may lay it in the center of the project, because you will not need to turn the papers over in order to pass the pieces back. This project, including the introduction, will take at least two periods.

Lesson 19: Winter Picture

Lesson Summary: Children will use crayons, markers, and white chalk on gray paper to create an expressive winter scene.

Purpose: Children will see how value affects their work, and the project will reinforce the concept of contrast.

Materials: 12″ × 18″ gray construction paper, crayons, markers, white chalk, pencils

Review: Value (definition), contrast (definition)

Time: One period

Possible Visual Aid: Pieter Breughel, *Hunters in the Snow*

This project is related to value and will reinforce the concept of contrast. You will need crayons, markers, pencils, white chalk, and 12″ by 18″ construction paper in some value of gray. I offer two choices, one light and one dark. If it is not technically winter when you present this project, or if you do not have wintry conditions in your state, adjust your introduction accordingly.

Ask the students what season of the year it is, and elicit the term "winter." Ask what images might appear in a picture that would let us know we were looking at a winter scene. Responses could include (but are not limited to) snow, bare trees, boots, mittens, heavy clothing, sleds, ice, icicles, snowballs, snow forts, smoke from chimneys, and so on. You might ask what holidays occur in winter and discuss possible images from Christmas, Hanukkah, Kwanza, or Valentine's Day.

Show the gray paper(s) and explain that each student will get a piece. Now, we all know that the winter sky can be a brilliant blue or the colors of a sunset, but for this project, we are going to use gray. This will not only offer contrast if the children want to draw snow, but it will make the picture look cold. An alternative is to use white paper and have children color the sky, perhaps using only pencil.

Put a piece of gray paper on the board and show how the white chalk shows up against it. As we discussed in Lesson 16, white chalk is much better than white crayon for this purpose. Ask what would happen if you used yellow marker to make a sun. The result will definitely be duller than if you drew on white. Demonstrate. The whole picture will look cold and somewhat dreary, even if you use bright colors. We want to emphasize the coldness of winter, and we want to see how the use of gray affects our colors.

Pass out the paper. Names go on the back in pencil, and the page may be turned either way. The students may draw anything that creates the feeling of winter. I discourage writing. I don't forbid it, but I explain that one of art's most important functions is to tell stories without words.

Lesson 20: File and Free

See Lesson 13.

Unit Three: **Texture**

The way something feels or appears to feel—its surface quality

Artists use texture in many different ways, so you have a wide variety of possible approaches to visual aids. You will be discussing the use of real texture, such as that found in bas relief, architecture, sculpture, or collage, so you should probably have some examples handy. This type of texture is all around you in the built environment, so you can always use your teaching space as an example. Carpet, brick, certain wallpapers, curtain fabric, acoustical ceiling tiles—the architectural applications are endless. You might discuss the practical applications of texture by having the children check the bottom of their shoes and describe what they find. Clothing designers also use contrasting textures, so a child might be wearing denim jeans and a fuzzy sweater.

You will also be discussing the illusion of texture, and it is very important to have at least one good visual aid to discuss. A painting in which the artist creates the realistic impression of a wide variety of textures is the most desirable. Some examples are Quentin Metsys' *Moneylender and His Wife*, works by William Harnett, or Martin Johnson Heade's *Cattleya Orchid and Three Brazilian Hummingbirds around Nest*. You might also have plastic laminate that looks like wood grain, or wallpaper that looks different than it feels.

You will want to have a great many real textures on hand as well. I have collected these for many years, but I have also purchased several sets of plastic rubbing plates from catalogs. You can cut these in half to serve more students. Since you will be using these for feeling and rubbing, not collage, they should last for many years. Be aware that you will get a different result depending on which side you use. You might also use textured wallpapers and a variety of materials found in hardware stores, such as sandpaper and screen door material. These should be relatively flat. If they are too spiky, they will tear the paper when the children create rubbings. I create an identical packet for each of my tables, putting the stack in an 8½″ by 11″ manila envelope, but your room configuration will determine your setup.

Lesson 21: Introducing Texture

Lesson Summary: Children will discuss the definition of "texture" and rub real surfaces to create the illusion of texture.

Purpose: Children will be introduced to the concept of texture and to two ways that artists use this element.

Materials: Visuals depicting real and illusory textures, a variety of real textures, 12″ × 18″ drawing paper, crayons, pencils (for name only)

Review: Elements of art

New Vocabulary/Concepts: Texture, real, illusion, surface, optical (optional)

Time: One period

Possible Visual Aids: Animal drawings by Albrecht Durer

Before class begins, place textures on each table. Ask the students what elements of art you have already studied, and then ask them if they can guess what element of art you are going to discuss today. When someone (hopefully) says "texture," put the word on the board and ask if anyone knows its definition. Usually somebody will refer to "feeling." Certainly, texture refers to the way something actually feels, and I start my definition with the words "The way something feels, or . . ." Then say, "Let's pretend I see a cat across the room. The cat appears to be furry, and of course, if I petted it, it would actually *feel* furry. But what if I see a very realistic painting of a cat?" (It would be terrific to have an appropriate visual aid. If you enter "cat painting" into a Web browser and search images, you'll find plenty. Be sure to pick one that looks very furry.) "That cat also looks furry, but if I were allowed to touch the painting (which, of course, I must never do!) would it feel furry? Of course not. It would feel like paint or chalk or whatever. But both the real cat and the painted cat exhibit texture." So you must add to the definition. "Texture is the way something feels or the way it appears to feel." Some people say it is the surface quality of something. Ask if anyone knows what the word "surface" means, and try to elicit the idea of "top" or "outside." Discuss some examples, like the surface of a pond or an ocean. In my class, I refer to the surface of our desks, which are plastic laminate, and explain that the inside is wood. I ask what is on the surface of our bodies, and everyone says "skin."

Explain that we can "feel things with our eyes," and that sometimes the way the surface appears is true, like the real cat, but sometimes it is an illusion, like the painting. Of course, you will then ask if anyone knows what an illusion is. Put this word on the board and discuss it. Perhaps your students have heard of optical illusions. If so, talk about "optical" as referring to our eyes. Define an "illusion" as "when we think we see something that isn't really there," such as water on the road or an oasis in the desert. Ask, "Other than an artist, what kind of person makes illusions?" Discuss the kinds of illusions a magician can create, and expand upon the idea that some art is a kind of illusion as well. Some artists are very good at creating the illusion of texture, and then tell them that that is what they are going to do today.

Put a piece of 12″ by 18″ white drawing paper on the board. If you don't have drawing paper, 11″ by 17″ computer paper or newsprint is fine. (Actually, construction paper will work, but thinner paper is better.) Place a texture from one of the tables under your paper and rub over it with a dark crayon, stressing the good frottage technique we discussed in Lesson 3. Explain that today they are only going to experiment, that you want them to use as many of the textures on the table as possible, so that next time, when they do make an actual artwork, they will have an idea of what is available. Each rubbed area should be about the size of their palm, so that they can get several on the paper. They may use any of the darker values, but they may only use crayon. Have them rub their fingers lightly over their results to see that it does not feel as real as it looks. They have used real textures to create illusions.

You might easily adapt this for older students by having them search the environment for their own textures rather than providing them. Or take your younger students on a "texture walk." If they rub textures on walls or floors, warn them to stay away from the edges of the paper.

Lesson 22:   Texture Illusion Draw and Fill

Lesson Summary: Children will create pictures using rubbed textures to fill the page.

Purpose: The project will introduce the concept of tessellation and reinforce the concept of textural illusion.

Materials: 12″ × 18″ white drawing paper, pencils (for names only), markers, crayons, textures

Review: Texture (definition), illusion, real

New Vocabulary/Concepts: Tessellation, repetition

Time: Five or six periods

Start with a brief review of the concepts. Ask what element was introduced last time, the definition of texture, what ways artists use textures, and so forth. Tell the students that in this project, they are going to rub the textures they experimented with during the previous lesson in order to create the illusion of texture.

There are two steps to this project, a marker drawing and texture rubbing. With younger children, it is a good idea to place the textures on the tables only after the drawings are done.

Place a piece of 12″ by 18″ white drawing paper on the board. Using markers, draw a picture or design that completely tessellates the page. As you draw, explain that they may draw a picture or design or a combination of both, but it must be tessellated. Discuss the concept of tessellation with the children. You might begin by asking if anyone knows what tessellation is. Students learn about tessellations in math class, and those models are relatively rigid. Tessellating a surface means covering a plane completely by repeating positive shapes that fit together in such a way that they leave no gaps. The ceramic tiles on many bathroom floors form tessellations, as do the squares on a checkerboard. Mosaics are tessellations. You might be able to point to the vinyl tiles on your classroom floor, or the acoustical ceiling tiles, or the windowpanes as examples of simple tessellations. If you want to incorporate math into this project, you could use it to introduce a lesson on tessellation, bringing in the works of M. C. Escher and making mathematical tessellations.

(See *Art Is Fundamental*, pp. 137–138.) Or simply explain that when you use the term in art class, it means that they are going to create a picture or design that has no big negative spaces, that divides the picture plane completely, like a puzzle. Demonstrate how they can divide a sky or a ground into tessellated shapes.

Explain that it is very important that their shapes not be too small, because they are going to fill each shape with a rubbed texture, and in order for people to see texture, there must be plenty of repetition. You might elaborate in the following way.

"If I have one grain of sand in my hand, is that a sandy texture? Two grains? Three? What if I have a handful of sand? There is no doubt that a handful of sand makes a texture. In order to create a texture, there must be lots of repetition. If I had one hair on my head, would that be a hairy texture?

Two hairs? Three? (You get the idea!) So we must have shapes that are big enough to allow for enough repetition to see the texture we are rubbing."

A student may use one or more marker colors for this drawing. Of course, darker colors will be more visible, but even yellow will work. It is very important that pupils remember not to fill in any of their shapes with marker. Everything must be outlined only.

When you have completed the shapes on your demonstration drawing, take a texture, place it under the paper, and fill one of the shapes by rubbing the texture with a crayon. Explain that the crayons they choose may or may not be the same color as the outlines, but that when they come to a marker line, they *must stop and change something.*

If you use something like the "tree—house—mountain—sun" image I describe in "Getting Started" for your demonstration, divide the crown of the tree into several shapes using a green marker. Fill one of the shapes with a texture using green crayon. Then ask, "If I want to keep my tree all green, and I must change something, what must it be?" Of course the answer is the texture, so demonstrate by placing a different texture under the shape next to the first one, and rub that with green as well. "But what if I like the texture I used first and want to use it for my whole tree, what could I do? That's right, I could change the color of my crayon." Demonstrate by filling several shapes with the same texture, but use a variety of crayon colors like orange and red-orange and blue-green. "I can change the texture or the color. What's my third choice? Of course, I can change both the color and the texture!" Demonstrate this as well.

Caution the children to avoid using very light crayons like pink, green-yellow, or orange-yellow. If a student forgets, she can go over that area with a darker value and the same texture. Very light colors won't show the texture from a distance. Explain that every shape must be filled, even things like clouds.

First graders Nytalia Patterson and Alexander Dall created these very different compositions filled with texture.

Lesson 23:   Real Textures—
Paper Fold and Crumble Montage

Lesson Summary: Children will use real textures they make from paper to create a montage (or bas relief).

Purpose: The project will reinforce the concept of artists using real textures in a work of art.

Materials: 12″ × 18″ construction paper in various colors, scissors, glue stick, pencils (for name and poking holes)

Review: Texture, illusion, real, collage, repetition

New Vocabulary/Concepts: Montage, bas relief (opt.)

Time: Three periods

Possible Visual Aids: Pre-Columbian or Hindu stone bas reliefs

For this project, you will need several colors of 12″ by 18″ construction paper, scissors, pencils, and glue. For older students, you might limit the class to white paper for a more sophisticated result.

Begin by asking what element of art the class has been studying, and by reviewing the definition of texture and some ways it is used by artists. Explain that in their last project, they created an illusion of texture, but this project will result in real textures. Select a color of construction paper and place it on the board. Cut a simple palm-sized shape from a separate sheet of the same color and glue it onto the first so that nothing sticks up. Ask the students if they can see the shape easily. Depending on the lighting in your room, it should be very difficult, if not impossible, to see where the piece is. (If you have some floodlights, you can create a situation where the little shadows at the edges disappear entirely.) Cut a second piece about the same size and shape as the first. Crumble it into a ball, open and flatten it, and then glue it onto the background paper, slightly overlapping the first piece. Ask if this piece is easy to see. Of course, the shadows will make it much more visible. Ask for other ways to texture paper. Using pieces about the same size and shape as the first two, create a variety of textures and glue them down, overlapping slightly each time. Some possibilities are small fan folds, poking holes with a sharp pencil or scissors (they'll need to be careful with this one), folding over and over sharply horizontally and then vertically for a waffle-like result, and fringing, as long as the fringes fill most of the piece. When you poke holes, be sure to put the glue on the smoother side of the piece. Another fun texture involves folding the paper, making small diagonal cuts on the fold, and then folding up the little "v" that results. Keep folding and cutting until the entire surface is covered with slits, then bend them all up.

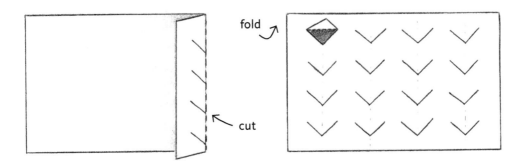

Explain to the students that they can create any texture they want, but they must think about the difference between a texture and a form. A piece of paper that is simply folded in half and glued down so that one half sticks up is not a texture. Review the concept of surface, and explain that whatever they do to the paper must cover most or all of the cut piece and should cast shadows of some sort. There needs to be a lot of repetition. If they poke holes in a piece, they must poke holes all over it, not just a few in the center. Use the sand analogy again (see previous lesson), and show some examples of incorrect solutions to the problem (like a piece of paper with little fringes on the edges but predominantly flat).

Explain that, while you created a simple design, they may cut shapes that make a picture. Flowers, trees, houses, dinosaurs, airplanes—the possibilities are endless. They may create any kind of picture or design they want, as long as the composition is good and their shapes are not too small. If the shape is too small, there can't be enough repetition to yield a texture. Remind them that the glue goes on the back of the cut piece, not on the background paper, and that the resulting project should be flat enough to fit in their portfolios.

Ask if anyone remembers the word for an artwork where things are attached to the background. Review the concept of collage (see Lesson 18), and explain that this project is a montage. You will explore the prefix "mono" at length in a future project, but you can point out that it means "one." A collage uses a collection of different materials, while a montage uses only one. Write the word on the board, and ask if anyone has ever seen a photomontage. Perhaps there is a montage of schoolwork or posters on the walls of your classroom or hall. Since the result of this project is somewhat sculptural, you might also discuss "bas relief." I have posters of bas reliefs on my wall, so it is easy to point out the similarities. (I always explain that the word is French, which is why the "s" is silent.)

Ask each child to select their favorite color from the available selection, give them *two* sheets of that color, and have them put their names in pencil on the front of one, small, in a corner. Remind them that that the pencils are only for writing names and poking holes, and they must only cut pieces from the sheet without their name. It is very easy to cut the wrong paper in this project. They may turn the paper either landscape or portrait, and they may overlap their pieces if they wish, however, it is a good idea to not overlap identical things, especially crumbled paper.

First grader Reni Osuntokun created this montage.

This project will take more than one period, and there may be small, unglued pieces to collect. At cleanup time, you might tell your students they are going to make a sandwich. The bottom of the sandwich is the background page, the "filling" is any unglued, cut piece, and the top of the sandwich is the rest of the second piece of paper, the one from which you are cutting your shapes. Make sure the filling is in the center of the background page.

Lesson 24: Paper Weaving— How Texture Relates to Pattern

Lesson Summary: Students will create paper weavings.

Purpose: Students will learn about various types of patterns and explore the relationship between pattern and texture.

Materials: 9″ × 12″ construction paper in several colors and values, 12″ × ½″ to ¾″ strips of construction paper in several colors and values, scissors, pencils (for names only), glue stick (optional)

Review: Texture (definition), repetition

New Vocabulary/Concepts: Pattern, random, regular, predict, weaving, warp, weft, woof, loom

Time: Three periods

Possible Visual Aids: Native American blankets

You will need several colors of construction paper for this project. If you start with 12″ by 18″ pieces, cut some into a 9″ by 12″ format. You will also need 12″ by ½″ to ¾″ strips, several of each color. A paper cutter is very helpful.

Begin by reviewing all the concepts that relate to texture: definition, how artists use it, real, illusion, and so forth. Explain that, while texture is an element of art, you are going to discuss a principle of art that is closely related.

A principle of art refers to how an artist uses the elements. Ask the students, "If I handed each of you a piece of black construction paper, some white string, four red circles, five blue squares, three yellow triangles, and a piece of rough fabric, and I told you to use them in a work of art, would all of your projects look alike? Of course not! Some of you might overlap your pieces. Some might use all the circles, creating repetition, while others might choose to use only one. Some might arrange their elements symmetrically, while others would scatter theirs. Things like balance and overlap and repetition are principles of art.

"The principle of art we are going to discuss today is pattern. A pattern occurs when there is enough repetition to predict what comes next. What does 'predict' mean? That's right, it's an educated guess about the future." Put "1, 0, ___" on the board, or a circle and a square, and ask the students what comes next. They can't really be sure, although they will guess. Now put "1,0,1,0,1,0,1,___" or "circle, square, triangle, circle, square, triangle, circle, square, ___" and ask the same thing. Because of the pattern that you have established, they will easily guess zero or a triangle. A pattern requires enough repetition to allow us to make an educated guess as to what comes next. You might discuss people who make predictions each day—like weathermen or women—and how repeated meteorological events allow them to see patterns, which in turn allow them to make guesses about the future.

There are two kinds of patterns you should discuss: regular patterns and random patterns. Start by asking what the word "random" means. Once you have elicited the information that it means "haphazard" or "unsystematic" or "in no particular order," you can ask how we could possibly have a random pattern. (You might discuss oxymorons here.) The concepts certainly seem contradictory. You might explain it this way: "Let's imagine I have a big canvas on the floor of my studio. I go outside and gather a huge armful of maple leaves, stand in front of my canvas and scatter them all over it. Wherever they fall, I trace around them. My canvas is so large, however, that I have about three feet on one end that is still empty. What must I do to finish my design?" When the students respond that you must gather more leaves and dump them over the empty part, ask, "What kind of leaves? Should I line them up?" A random pattern does not allow us to predict specifically, but it does allow us to predict generally. They know that your design will continue with maple leaves and that they will be scattered. If you look around the room, you will usually find several children wearing patterns. Some, like stripes, will be very regular. Some, like many floral patterns, are seemingly random. Point to each appropriate garment and ask, "Random or regular?"

Once you have established the concept of pattern, ask how patterns and textures are similar—what do they have in common? Repetition. Remember the discussion of sandy and hairy textures in Lesson 22? Review this concept and discuss the fact that if we look at a texture under a microscope, it would create a pattern. Pick a simple texture your students have used and hold it up. Then draw it on the board, using a much bigger scale. The result will be a regular or random pattern.

Look around the room at the clothes the children are wearing. Some fabrics are patterned but flat—the pattern is printed on the surface or woven in such a way that there is no texture change. In other cases, the pattern creates a texture, as in certain knits. Or you might say the texture creates a pattern. Different fabrics will suggest different possibilities. Discuss the different possibilities: the pattern and texture are separate, the pattern creates the texture, the texture creates the pattern, and so forth. You might have an old sweater or afghan on hand, just to be on the safe side.

Once you have illustrated the point, talk a little about weaving. Explain that some fabrics are woven, and that there are different patterns used in weaving. You are going to use the simplest: over one and under one. Discuss the fact that weaving is done on a loom and that the lengthwise fibers are called the "warp," while the crosswise fibers are called the "woof" or "weft." In this project, you are going to use a paper loom that will also serve as the warp lines. Your wefts will also be made from paper.

Begin the project by demonstrating the process. Hamburger fold a piece of 9″ by 12″ construction paper. Hold the still-folded page so that the fold is *at the bottom*. Coming in about an inch or so from one side, cut from the bottom fold up, stopping about an inch from the top. Move your scissors over about an inch from the last cut and make a similar cut. Repeat the process until you are within an inch or so from the other edge. These cuts can be straight or curvy or zigzag. They can create a regular or random pattern. The important thing is that the cuts don't come too close to each other or to the edges of the paper. Keep stressing that the cuts must begin only on the folded edge. (Rather than use an inch as your measure, you could tell the students to use the distance between two knuckles on a finger.)

The strips should be placed in an easily accessible place, organized into stacks by color (or value, in the case of black, white, and gray). Select a few strips that contrast highly with your loom. Demonstrate weaving the strips into the loom using an "over one, under one" technique. Show the students that because of this pattern, two strips of the same color can be used next to each other. In the actual project, students may use strips from up to five different stacks. That is, they might use strips from only one or two stacks, but no more than five different kinds. This will ensure some sort of pattern. None of the strips should exactly match the background. Make sure the weaving is tight—that is, don't leave spaces between the strips. They should touch corner to corner. Of course, some of the strip will hang over each end. You might give your students a choice about these fringes. They could leave them, or trim them even with the edges of the loom. With young children, you might choose to do the trimming yourself, depending on how straight you want the results to be. If the students want the fringes cut, it is a good idea to use a little glue to keep them from sliding out.

This project takes more than one period for young children. If the loom still folds in the middle, have students place unused strips in the center and close the loom on the original fold. They should place their names, small, on an outside corner near a flap (not a corner near the fold). If the piece is woven tightly and no longer folds, just have the weaver lay any extra strips on top and place his or her name in a corner.

First grader Adam Miller created this lovely weaving.

For older students, there are wonderful variations on paper weaving (consult a book or the Web), or perhaps you might be able to use real looms and yarn, or grasses, strips of recyclables, like newspaper, trash bags, and so forth.

Lesson 25: A Texture Has a Special Look

Lesson Summary: Students will draw the same image using four different media.

Purpose: Children will think about the different textures and effects of various media and how they feel to use.

Materials: 12″ × 18″ white construction paper, pencils, black markers (thick or thin line), black crayons, charcoal (pencil or vine)

Review: Texture

New Vocabulary/Concepts: Medium

Time: One period

Possible Visual Aids: Works in various media: a pen drawing, a painting, a pastel, a sculpture, etc.

If a copy exists in your local library, start by reading *A Picture Has a Special Look* by Helen Borten. This is a wonderful introduction to the concept that different media have different textures. If time allows, and depending upon the age of the student, you might begin by reading it to the class.

You will need pencils, black markers, black crayons, and charcoal, as well as 12″ by 18″ white construction paper. (For younger children, I would pass the charcoal out only when it is needed.) Begin by explaining that artists use different media. Media is the plural of medium. (Write this on the board.) Ask if anyone knows what the word "medium" means. Usually, students will refer to something that's "not too big and not too little," and of course, this is one meaning of the word. Discuss some examples of this—not too hot or cold, not too tall or short, not too dark or light, and so forth—before explaining that there is another use of the term, that also means "in the middle," or "in between," but in a very different way.

Tell the students that you are thinking of a fabulous work of art you are going to create. The colors and shapes are terrific, and it has wonderful textures. Can they see it? Of course not, because it's only in your head. What must you do to make it visible to them? They will only be able to see it when you actually create the work out of materials, like paint or wood or stone or crayon. The different materials artists use are called "media." The medium is the means by which an artist gets his or her idea across to the viewer. It is "in between" the artist and the viewer.

Have the students name some media. Paper, crayon, marker, ink, colored pencil, regular pencil, tempera paint, oil paint, watercolor, marble, plaster, wire—the possibilities are pretty endless. Explain that there are other uses for the word as well. You might discuss movies about people who contact the spirit world, like *Poltergeist* or *Ghost*. A medium is what we call the person who acts as the middleman, so to speak, between the spirits and physical world. "The media" is also how we refer to the various ways of transmitting news and information and entertainment to the public. Radio, television, newspapers, periodicals, and movies are all considered media. The medium is the physical way that one person sends ideas to another. It exists in the middle between the two.

In art, different media look and feel different. This project will focus on the various textures implied by alternate materials.

Give each student a piece of 12″ by 18″ white construction paper. Have them put their names on one side in pencil. Have them fold their paper in half hamburger fold, then open the page and fold it again hot dog fold. This should divide the page into quarters. Each student should then place his or her paper on the desk in either landscape or portrait orientation with the blank side up.

Have them pick up the pencils. Explain that they are going to draw a picture or design *in one quarter only*. They should make it interesting, but simple enough to be copied three more times. Divide the time left in the period by four and explain that they will have about that much time to finish this section. They should think about things they can do with a pencil, like shading or gradation. Normal pencils cannot make deep black values, but they can make a wide variety of values and they can make very precise lines and small details. Encourage the students to use these properties in this section.

When the allotted time is up, students who are not finished with the pencil drawing may keep working, but they should listen carefully. Have the other students pick up the black crayons. In any blank quarter, they should copy the image in the first section as carefully as possible. Discuss the differences and similarities between the two media. A crayon can create a much deeper black than a pencil, but it cannot generate as sharp a line. Like the pencil, it can create gradation. Have the students think about how different the crayon feels from the pencil—it is a smoother, waxier medium.

When you move on to the marker, once again point out the differences and similarities. Like the crayon, the marker can create a deep black. If you are using a thin marker, it can make a precise line like a pencil. But unlike the first two media, it cannot create gradation by adjusting the pressure. The students will have to find a different way to approximate shading, like crosshatching or short, sketchy lines or stippling. Once again, call attention to the way it feels to draw with this medium.

In the final quarter, the students will copy the image with charcoal. Caution them about smearing. They can use this quality to create gradation, but it can also cause problems. Contrast and compare this medium with the others. Lines are not sharp and precise, the black is a different quality, you can create gradation, and it feels very different when you use it.

After all four sections are complete, ask students which medium they liked using best. Explain that artists frequently prefer some media over others. If they were going to draw a furry cat, which material might they choose and why? What if they were making a design for a piece of scientific equipment? A landscape?

First grader Elise Grandlund used four different media in this charming drawing.

This project is extremely adaptable to older students. Simply have them create a gridded work that features the same image using a variety of materials. These might include regular pencil, pen, marker, charcoal, tempera, watercolor, torn or cut paper, oil pastel, acrylic, printmaking, colored pencil, or any other medium you can think of.

Lesson 26: File and Free

See Lesson 13.

Unit Four: **Shape**

A two-dimensional, or flat, closed figure

Using poster board in a variety of colors, cut out a large number of geometric shapes, such as circles, squares, triangles, rectangles, and parallelograms. These should not be too big or too little. My circles have diameters of 2″, 2½″, and 3″. My squares have 1″, 2″, and 3″ sides. My rectangles are 2″ by 5½″, 1″ by 3″, and 1″ by 2″. I have equilateral, oblique, isosceles, and right triangles in similar sizes and some small parallelograms. Be sure that some of your shapes are white or gray or black. Since I have four tables, I have at least four of each size and shape, and I keep the sets in separate envelopes.

Quilts make terrific visual aids for shape units. You can use pictures, but real quilts would be even better. Virtually every culture has art that uses shapes of some sort. Depending on what your class is studying in social studies, you might look for the shapes in that culture's art. Islamic tiles, for example, would work well, or comparing the shapes of letters from different alphabets. Or go through picture books and look for specific shapes. As you will see, math class is an excellent resource for visuals for the beginning of this unit.

Lesson 27: **Introducing Shape**

Lesson Summary: Students will discuss the nature of shapes and discuss geometric shapes.

Purpose: Students will start to become sensitive to the effect of various kinds of shapes in a work of art.

Materials: Cardboard cutouts of various geometric shapes

Review: Color, value, texture (name and define)

New Vocabulary/Concepts: Shape, two-dimensional, enclosed, geometric, geometry, length, width, depth, dimension, circle, square, triangle, rectangle, parallelogram, pentagon, hexagon, septagon, octagon, nonagon, decagon, oval, five-pointed star, six-pointed star, semicircle, crescent, trapezoid

Time: One period

Place a set of shapes on each table. Spread them out so that they can be easily seen. Ask the students what element of art they think they will be focusing on today. (They should all guess shape.) You might want to ask what elements they have already studied, just to review the idea of elements.

Ask for the definition of shape. Even though I initially present this question to first graders, they are aware that shapes are two-dimensional and enclose an area. Demonstrate the difference between flat, two-dimensional, and three-dimensional. I usually lead a somewhat lengthy discussion about the difference between something that is merely flat and something that is truly two-dimensional. I draw a shape on the board and try to pick it up off the surface. Of course I can't, because it is truly two-dimensional. Anything that can be picked up or casts a shadow is actually three-dimensional, but for the purposes of art class, very flat objects are considered two-dimensional. You will hear artists refer to canvas and paper—materials where we only consider the front surface—as two-dimensional media. After discussing dimensions, ask what the dimensions are, and elicit height or length, width, and depth or thickness. You might say, "If I lie down on a piece of paper and someone traces me, they have drawn my shape, but if they make a sculpture of me, it will have height and width and depth." Show different kinds of paper and cardboard to display the different thicknesses, and explain that if pieces of paper were truly two-dimensional, you could stack thousands of them without seeing any depth to the pile. The idea of an enclosed area can be demonstrated by drawing a line that does not connect to the point where it began and then connecting—or closing—it. No matter how large a shape is, I can follow it all the way around and come back to where I started. Thus every shape is a flat, or two-dimensional, closed figure. Write the definition on the board.

The next question involves much higher level thinking skills. Ask the children to look at the cardboard pieces on the table and tell you what all the shapes have in common. It is best to start with some givens. You are going to agree that they are all shapes, so they are all closed figures and they are all flat. Write "shapes," "flat," and "closed" on the board. Also agree that they are all cardboard and add that to the list. Then ask for answers. Not all the shapes have corners or sides, and if a child replies that they all have color, point out the white or black or gray shapes. With older students, someone might well respond that they are all geometric shapes, but with younger children, you want to elicit the fact that they all have names. If this doesn't happen in a reasonable length of time, ask them to tell you specifically what's on the table. They should say circles, squares, triangles, and so forth, and that should allow you to draw out the idea of names.

When someone says "square," we all think of a shape that has four equal sides and four right angles. When someone says "circle," we all think of a shape where every point on the circumference is equally distant from the center. (You should draw these examples on the board.) So not only do these shapes have names, they also have rules that we learn about in math class. If you say "cloud," some people might think of stratus clouds, some might envision cirrus, and others cumulus formations. Probably no two people would form exactly the same image in their minds. But while I might think of a big square and you might think of a little one, the word will always elicit the same shape, following the rules cited. Triangles do have variations, but they all have three sides and three angles that add up to 180 degrees. Because the kind of math that deals with these shapes is called geometry, we call these geometric shapes. Ask the students to name as many geometric shapes as possible and list the answers on the board.

Explain that not all shapes have names. Draw a blobby shape on the board and ask if it is a shape. Several students will probably say no. Counter this with, "Is it closed? (Yes.) Is it two-dimensional? (Yes.) Then it's a shape. We will explore that kind of figure later."

Lesson 28:   Geometric Shape

Lesson Summary: Students will create a colorful design or picture using geometric shapes.

Purpose: Students will learn about positive and negative shape and reinforce their knowledge of geometric shape. Students will also improve their small muscle control.

Materials: Cardboard geometric shapes, 12″ × 18″ (or 9″ × 12″) white construction paper, pencils, black markers, oil pastels (or crayons)

Review: Geometric shape, overlap

New Vocabulary/Concepts: Positive and negative shape, composition (optional)

Time: Five or six periods

Possible Visual Aids: Later works by Piet Mondrian or Vasily Kandinsky; works by Victor Vasarely

For this project, you will need the cardboard shapes you created, pencils, black markers, and oil pastels. If you do not have oil pastels, crayons will do. You will begin the lesson with a review of the vocabulary introduced in the last class: shape (its definition) and the kind of shapes that are on the table (geometric, or shapes with names).

Hold up a piece of 12″ by 18″ white construction paper, and explain that each student will trace the cardboard shapes onto the paper to create a picture or design. (If time is a factor, 9″ by 12″ paper will work as well.)

On the board, draw a fairly large rectangle to represent a piece of paper. Draw a shape of some sort in the center of the rectangle, and ask how many shapes you have created. Some students will answer "one," but several should realize that you have actually made two shapes. Explain that the shape you drew inside the rectangle is called the "positive" shape, and the shape that we might call the background is called "negative" space. One of the goals of this project is to create a composition in which we cannot tell the difference between positive and negative spaces.

Instead of doing an actual paper and pencil demonstration at this point, once again draw a large rectangle on the board to represent the paper. On this rectangle, trace some of the geometric shapes. (If you have a whiteboard, be careful not to get marker on the cardboard.) This will make the example easier to see. Explain that the students will do this step in pencil. Be sure to overlap, and have some of the shapes extend over the edge of the rectangle.

Look at the shapes you have created. Are they all geometric? No. How is this possible, when you have only traced geometric shapes?

There are three reasons that you will have nongeometric shapes on the page. First of all, when your shapes overlap, you may or may not create a geometric shape. Secondly, when a shape goes off the page, the shape left on the page might not be geometric. And most importantly for this discussion, you might surround negative spaces that are not geometric.

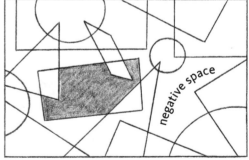

Demonstrate these possibilities. The student is to compose the page in such a way that none of the shapes is obviously negative. The result should be the kind of tessellation we discussed in Lesson 22. The students may produce recognizable imagery like a robot, truck, train, house, or tree, or simply create a design. When shapes overlap, the resulting shapes should not be too small. Encourage good composition: students should not overlap excessively in one area or leave another spot too empty.

Pass out paper and have the children put their names on the back. After they have created a composition by tracing the shapes with pencil, they should go over the pencil lines carefully with black marker. (Both of these exercises, especially the tracing, help young children develop their fine motor skills.) When a student or two is ready for the next step, demonstrate the use of oil pastel. Remind them that different media have different properties, and one of the special things about oil pastel is its velvety richness. Draw some geometric shapes on white paper with black marker, being sure to overlap. Color each new shape carefully with rich, solid oil pastel. Explain that no two shapes that share a side may be colored with the same pastel. Stress the fact that when a student comes to a marker line, they must stop and change their pastel. If they have overlapped circles to make the crown of a tree, they might merely change from true green to dark green to yellow-green to grayed green. Or they could go from orange to purple, but they must change pastels. Negative shapes are treated just like positive shapes. No shapes will be left uncolored. Students may use any oil pastel except black, and they may mix colors and values, although this will take more time. If you use crayons, you might use them thickly to approximate oil pastels, or encourage contrast and gradation.

First grader Josh Parquet composed this terrific geometric shape project.

This lesson works well for older students. If you are condensing the three years and have already covered color schemes, you could easily ask the students to select a color scheme for this project. For students of any age, this lesson will take several periods. Simply begin each period with a review of the vocabulary and rules.

Note: If time allows, you could ask younger students to sort the shapes during each cleanup rather than simply gathering them into a pile. This will add an extra dimension to the project.

Lesson 29: **Irregular and Organic Shape**

Lesson Summary: Students will create a cut-paper montage using irregular and organic shapes.

Purpose: Students will learn about irregular and organic shapes. They will start to see that artworks that use geometric shapes have a different look than those with nongeometric shapes.

Materials: 12″ × 18″ construction paper in various colors and black, scissors, pencils, glue

On each table, place a stack of various bright colors of construction paper, pencils, scissors, and glue. Place the construction paper on a page of opened newspaper. Have the students place the scraps of leftover paper flatly on the newspaper during cleanup, and simply stack the piles. Use the same paper for this project and the next, and simply add replacement colors as needed.

After a brief review of the element of art (shape), its definition (a flat, closed figure), and the kind of shape (geometric) that you have been covering, hold up a piece of paper, and explain that there is a shape hiding in it. Cut an extremely *non*geometric shape out of the piece. Ask if, in fact, this is a shape. If some children say no, ask, "Is it flat? Is it closed?" Of course it is both these things, so it is a shape. You might discuss the following scenario. "Let's say Mom goes to the hospital to have a baby. The doctors told her she was having a girl, so she had a girl's name all picked out. But, lo and behold, she has a boy, and she doesn't have any boys' names in mind. Does that mean her son is not a baby because he doesn't have a name? Of course not! It looks like a baby, it cries like a baby, it wets like a baby—it has all the properties of a baby, so it is a baby. Just because our shape doesn't have a name doesn't mean it's not a shape. We don't want to hurt its feelings, so let's call him Murgatroyd. Say 'hi' to Murgatroyd! Shapes like Murgatroyd don't have names or rules, but they are still shapes, because they are flat and closed. We have two ways of referring to such shapes. They can be 'organic' or 'irregular.'" Write these words on the board.

Focus on the word "organic." Ask if anybody knows what an organ is (not the kind you play music on). Have the class list as many as they can, and write them on the board. Then ask, "What kinds of things have organs?" They will probably start listing various animals—or plants. If no one gets the idea, add a few prompts. "Do mountains have organs? Do rocks? Does this table?" Elicit the idea that living things have organs. We call shapes that look like living, growing things "organic." Draw a shape something like an amoeba on the board and ask if any of the students know what an amoeba is. Explain briefly. Then draw a very jagged shape with sharp edges. Explain that, while it does not look like a living thing, it also has no names or rules; however, it is a two-dimensional, closed figure. We call shapes like this "irregular." Write the word on the board and underline the "ir." Explain that this prefix means "not." You might ask for other words that begin with "ir," like "irreversible," or "irresponsible."

Place a piece of 12″ by 18″ black construction paper on the board. Cut a very irregular or organic shape out of a highly contrasting paper, like yellow, and glue it onto the black. Repeat this with red or green or orange, and overlap the first shape. Demonstrate that when they overlap shapes cut from the same piece of paper, it just looks like one bigger shape. Explain that they are going to fill the page with organic and irregular shapes. When they overlap, they should not create geometric shapes, and they are welcome to leave negative black spaces showing, but they should not be geometric either. They are welcome to create a picture or design. Remind them to put the glue on the back of the piece they are gluing down, not on the black background. Encourage them to cut freely. They are not to draw the shape first. (You might remove the pencils after names are on the papers.)

For older students (or even younger ones), you might set up an organic still life, like plants, and have them interpret it in cut paper. On this project, the names go on the front of the black paper, small, in a corner. This lesson usually takes more than one period, so a student may place unglued, cut pieces in the center of the project and you will not have to turn it over to find the name when handing them back.

Lesson 30: Related Shapes

Lesson Summary: Children will create a cut-paper montage using related shapes.

Purpose: The lesson will reinforce the concept of related shapes. Children will be sensitized to related shapes in art.

Materials: 12″ × 18″ construction paper, many colors plus white, pencils (for names only), scissors, glue sticks, crayons and/or markers

Review: Shape (definition), positive, negative, geometric, irregular, organic, overlap

New Vocabulary/Concept: Related shape

Time: Two+ periods

Possible Visual Aid: Van Gogh's *Still Life: Vase with Fifteen Sunflowers*, 1888

This lesson will require essentially the same materials as the last one, but instead of black construction paper, you will need white for the background. You may add black paper to the stacks on the tables. You will also need crayons and/or markers.

Begin with the usual review. After discussing the element, its definition, the kinds of shapes you have covered, and so forth, put something like the arrangement shown here on the board and ask which one does not belong. (Be aware that some students will disagree on the answer. Some will focus on the general shapes and some on the curved quality.) Most children have encountered problems like this on standardized tests. Use as many examples as you need to get the point across.

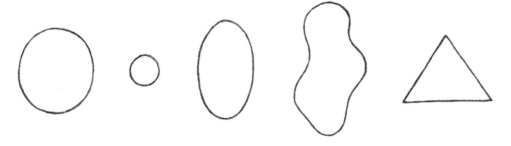

Discuss the nature of relationships. You might ask if any of your students have been told they look or sound like another member of their family, or share some other trait. Unless they have an identical twin, they will not look exactly like anyone else. When an artist uses exactly the same shape (or color or texture) more than once, we call that repetition. But when an artist uses shapes (or colors or textures) that are similar but not identical, we call those shapes "related." Using related shapes helps tie the artwork together. At this point, you might turn to a visual aid such as Vincent Van Gogh's *Still Life: Vase with Fifteen Sunflowers*, painted in 1888. You can find myriad images of this painting online. It is filled with circles and ovals. If you obtain a copy and laminate it, you could use a dry erase marker to actually draw on the flowers and emphasize all of these related shapes. You might point out that Van Gogh used related colors as well.

Explain that the students are going to create a picture or design that uses related shapes by cutting those shapes and gluing them on to a white background. On the board, draw a rectangle to represent a piece of paper. Place it in the landscape position. Create an example something like the following.

"Let's say the first shape I cut out is a triangle of some sort." (See Figure 1.) "Once I have cut out a shape, I must

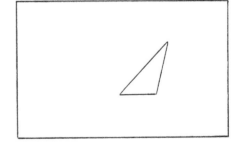

Figure 1

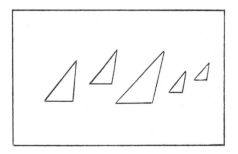

Figure 2

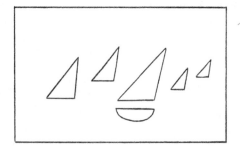

Figure 3

Figure 4

cut out *at least* four more shapes that are related to it. Not identical, just similar. They can be cut from the same paper or totally different colors." Add four more triangles. (See Figure 2.) "Once I have a total of at least five related shapes, I can change to a new shape. I'm going to add one like this." (See Figure 3.) "Now I must add at least four more related to that one." (See Figure 4.)

"Then I can move on to another shape. My shapes can be geometric or organic. Remember, I must have *at least* five of each kind of shape, but I can have many more. In this project, unlike our last one, once you have filled your page in an interesting way, you may add details with markers or crayons."

Draw a large rectangle on the board in the portrait position. Explain that, while the project can involve several different kinds of shapes, it can also be created from one basic shape. Draw something like the image shown here.

This project will take more than one period. As in the previous lesson, have the children put their names on the front of the background paper, small, in pencil. Since this project and the last require similar materials, and since some children will not finish in the allotted time, you might pass back both projects for a catch-up period.

Lesson 31:   Cloud Shapes—Using Imagination

Lesson Summary: Students will create a picture based upon an unusually shaped scrap of paper left over from previous projects.

Purpose: This project challenges the child's imagination. It also reinforces concepts of positive and negative shape.

Materials: 12″ × 18″ white construction paper, colored construction paper scraps from previous lessons, glue sticks, markers and/or crayons, pencils (for names only)

Review: Shape (definition), geometric, organic, irregular, positive, negative

New Vocabulary/Concept: Imagination

Time: One period

After the previous two lessons, you should have many colorful scraps of left-over paper in very irregular shapes. Select enough of these so that each student can have one, with a few extra. You might have to cut some of these apart or trim them. Each shape should be good-sized, but not huge, and have an interesting contour.

After the usual review, discuss the idea of imagination. Ask students if they have ever seen clouds in the sky that looked like things—planes, rabbits, flowers? Explain that they are going to do something similar. Hold up one of the scrap pieces, and tell them that they are each going to get one. They may turn it in any direction and use either side. Once they have found an image in the shape, they will glue it onto a piece of 12″ by 18″ white construction paper and use crayons or markers to finish the picture. This should be a very free project, but I do have one rule. If the student gets a red shape, let's say, he or she can't take a red marker or crayon and fill in all the irregular edges to make a rectangle or oval or some completely different shape. They can add tails or ears or other protrusions, but the original shape must be clearly visible. You will have to use your own judgment about small adjustments. The idea is to challenge the student's imagination, and allowing the pupil to completely transform the shape doesn't accomplish that. Encourage them to look at both the positive shape and its negative aspects. Sometimes it is the chunk missing from one side of a piece that becomes the focal point: a tunnel or the head of a duck. Children are welcome to draw on the colored piece. They may add spots to a dog or windows to a castle. Remind them that this is their own work. You want to know what they see in a shape, not what their neighbor sees. If they struggle for more than five minutes, or get too frustrated, you can offer them an alternative scrap. This project can be just as challenging for older students.

Lesson 32:   File and Free

See Lesson 13.

Lesson 33:   Spring Picture

Lesson Summary: Children will draw a picture expressing spring.

Purpose: The project will reinforce the concept that each artist is unique, and it will also reinforce the nature of the artistic process.

Materials: 12″ × 18″ white construction paper, crayons and/or markers, pencils, drawing boards (if drawing outside)

Review: Unique, what artists do, possibly shape

Time: One period

Possible Visual Aids: Various spring-themed paintings by Grant Wood

If the time of year is right, you might do a seasonal project at this point. Since the curriculum included a fall and winter picture, a spring picture is appropriate as well. While this project does not fit into a particular unit, as did fall and winter, it reinforces the concept that we introduced in Lesson 2, that one of the things we discuss in art class is how artists see the world, and that each artist is unique. And you could certainly focus on the shapes of the things the children draw. Beyond curricular concerns, it gives the children a chance to draw a little more freely than some of the recent projects. If you have the right conditions, this is a great opportunity to incorporate some observational drawing—especially if flowers are budding outside or you can see trees. You can also observe the students' progress by comparing the three seasonal pictures.

Ask the students what season of the year it is. After eliciting "spring," ask what kinds of things you might see in a spring picture. What subject matter might an artist choose to let the viewers know it is spring without using words? When the students have suggested enough possibilities to give everyone some good ideas, simply remind each student that no two projects should look alike, pass out paper, and begin. (Or go outside and draw what you see.)

Unit Five: **Line**

The path of a moving point

Artists use line in a wide variety of ways. Lines may be real or implied, thick or thin, curved, jagged, or straight—the possibilities are endless. They show us direction and movement. Almost any drawing, sketch, or etching would make a good visual aid. We will be discussing contour lines, calligraphic lines, outlines, and so forth.

Lesson 34: Introduction to Line

Lesson Summary: After discussing the nature of a line, students will draw an image using a pencil.

Purpose: Children will learn the definition of a line and use a variety of lines to create an image.

Materials: 12″ × 18″ white drawing or construction paper, pencils

Review: Color, shape, texture, value, dimensions, length, width, thickness or depth

New Vocabulary/Concepts: Line (definition), point, movement (descriptive words)

Time: One period

Possible Visual Aids: Naum Gabo, *Linear Construction*; architectural drawings; Pablo Picasso, *Dove of Peace* or *Columbe avec Flerus*

Before beginning your discussion of line, review the elements of art, including the definitions of the ones you have already covered. Ask if anyone knows the definition of "line." Depending on the age of your students, someone may give you the mathematical definition. In plane geometry, a line is straight, one dimensional, and infinite. In solid geometry, it may be curved. Even my first graders know that a line in math is one dimensional and infinite. At the very least, if you draw a line on the board, your students will probably know it's a line when they see it. Explain that the definition we are going to use in art may also work for math, although actual lines in art have many differences.

For art purposes, we are going to define line as "the path of a moving point." To elicit this definition from younger students, try the following. Place your chalk or marker on the board, and make a dot. Ask the children what we call that figure. They will offer several responses, including dot, circle, spot, period, and so forth. If no one says "point," write something like 2.3 on the board. Someone will say "point."

Place a point on the board, and let the children see it. Then put your marker back on the point and move it in a long path back and forth along the board. Move your body along the path as you move the marker. That is, don't just stand in one spot and move your hand or arm. As you walk, ask the students what you are doing. Elicit the fact that you are moving. Try not to cross the resulting line in any way; stop and ask the children what the point did and what it created. The point moved and created the line.

Offer something like the following. "Our 'point' was really a tiny circle. It had two dimensions. In math, a point has no dimensions. In math a line has one dimension." (You might want to review the meaning of "dimension.") "We cannot see things that have less than two dimensions, and while we sometimes refer to implied lines in art, we are usually referring to the ones we see. In math, lines go on forever, but in art, they don't." (Here you might discuss a line segment.) "In art, lines have length and width, otherwise we couldn't see them. We can even talk about lines, in things like wire sculptures, which have three dimensions. Lines send our eyes *moving* in certain *directions*. We'll talk more about that later. Because drawn lines have two dimensions, we can talk about wide lines and narrow lines." Draw as many different kinds of lines as you can think of on the board and ask students to describe them. Curvy, straight, jagged, thick, thin, curlicue, angular, broken—if you can draw it, they should be able to find a word or words to describe it.

Explain that they are essentially going to do a free drawing, but you would like them to do it with lines. When a line goes back to where it started, it creates a shape, but it is still a line. (We call it an "outline" and we will talk more about those later as well.) So they are welcome to use shapes, but encourage them to use lines *as* lines as well. They are going to use a pencil for this project; therefore, they can make small details if they want to. Ask them to make as many different kinds of lines as they can. They may draw a picture or a design and turn their paper in either direction.

Lesson 35: Line as Direction

Lesson Summary: Students will create a picture or design using cut-paper lines.

Purpose: Students will discover the way line creates movement in art.

Materials: 12″ × 18″ construction paper in various colors, black, and white, colored construction paper strips, glue stick, pencils (for names only), access to a paper cutter, scissors (optional)

Review: Line (definition), dimension

New Vocabulary/Concepts: Direction, movement, horizontal, vertical, diagonal

Time: One or two periods

Possible Visual Aids: Jasper Johns's *Three Flags*, Shosun's *Birds in Bamboo Tree*, works by Piet Mondrian, such as *Composition, 1913*

Before class, cut many, many "lines" from 12″ by 18″ colored construction paper, using a paper cutter. Place two or three sheets of a color on the cutter until a tiny amount hangs over the edge and slice. Your results should be various widths, although none of them should be more than ⅜″ or so. They can be 12″ or 18″ long. Put piles of multicolored "lines" on each table, with pencils and glue sticks.

Review the concept of "line" including the definition. Discuss the fact that our lines are really very thin shapes, because they have two dimensions, but when a shape in an artwork is thin enough and long enough, we see it as a line. Remind them that art lines can come in many varieties, but today they are going to focus on straight lines. Draw a straight line on the board. Point out that it tends to make our eyes run along its length. You might draw an arrow and discuss its similar effect.

Draw several horizontal, parallel lines. Ask the students to describe the effect. Then draw several vertical lines and discuss them. Draw some diagonal lines and repeat the exercise. Finally, draw a bunch of lines that crisscross and go in many directions. Horizontal lines tend to be calmer—like people sleeping, or the flat ground. Vertical lines tend to be livelier, like people standing up or trees growing. Diagonal lines can move in and out of the picture plane more than horizontal or vertical ones. The more directions in which our eyes are led, the more active the composition.

This is a fairly simple project. Each student will get a piece of 12″ by 18″ construction paper. Black or white will work best, but you could offer a choice of colors as well, with the proviso that the students not use lines of the same color as their background. The children will make a picture or design by gluing the lines on to the paper. Be sure that they put the glue on the line, not on the background. They can simply pull the strip across the top of the glue stick. If you use liquid glue, place newspaper at each student's place and have them use a paintbrush to apply glue to the back of the strips. They may cut or tear the strips to shorter lengths. If you feel this will take more than one period, have students put their names on the front of the project.

Lesson 36:   A Class Coloring Book

Lesson Summary: Each student will create a personal page for a class coloring book.

Purpose: Students will learn about outlines and contour lines and practice using them.

Materials: 8½″ × 11″ white (computer) paper, pencils, black markers, access to a copy machine

Review: Line (definition), shape (definition), negative space

New Vocabulary/Concepts: Outline, contour

Time: Two periods

Possible Visual Aids: Medieval manuscript illuminations, which usually have black contour lines around the shapes, or Egyptian wall paintings or papyrus illustrations for the same reason. Possibly some actual coloring books.

After the usual review, draw a shape on the board. Discuss the fact that, even though you closed it to make a shape, they can still see the line you used. Ask them if anyone knows what we call this kind of line, the kind that shows us the shape of something. It is called an outline, and we frequently make outlines with contour lines.

Ask if anyone knows the meaning of the word "contour." "Contour refers to the shape or form of something. We talk about the contour of a car, or the contours of our bodies.

"In art, a contour line is a line that never gets wider or narrower. It is not a sketchy line or a 'lost and found' line." On the board, create an ambling line with an even pressure of your chalk or marker. The line should stay uniform in width. Show the difference between this and a sketchy line. If possible, create the kind of line used in calligraphy, and compare it to your contour line.

Explain that the project they are going to do involves both of these meanings of contour line. They are going to make a coloring book. Before we continue, I'd like to say a few words about coloring books.

Calligraphic

Contour

Sketchy

In some circles, coloring books have gotten a very bad name. These are often the same circles that encourage kids to color outside the lines. As an art teacher, of course I am in favor of creativity. Solving a visual problem in a personal and unique way should be the goal of every artist, and the best art projects offer students an opportunity to do just that. And I would never recommend an art program that relied on fill-in-the-shape handouts. I think my curriculum speaks for itself. However, I have absolutely nothing against coloring books, as long as children also have plenty of blank paper on which to express their own ideas. Certain studies have shown that very young children may even learn to formulate visual concepts through the simplified drawings in coloring books. And as an art teacher, I certainly believe in coloring *in* the lines. It's what I call craftsmanship. Rembrandt colored in the lines, and so did Picasso. The trick for an artist is to know when to color in the lines and when to go beyond them, and of course, artists create their own lines. But by first grade, every child should be capable of staying in the lines if they try, and that's where coloring books can be very helpful. A friend of mine had an illness as a child, and one of her therapies was using coloring books to retrain her small muscles. Young children certainly need to develop fine motor skills for a number of reasons, so things like tracing and rubbing and coloring in are very helpful. Coloring in the lines needn't stifle a child's creativity. A cow could be colored purple or polka-dotted or striped, so restrictions need not be excessive. Of course, I'm not in favor of criticizing a child's coloring book style even if they scribble, but a parent can at least judge the development of muscle control by observing the improvement of technique during these early years. Depending upon your population, you might discuss some of these issues with your students. While the use of coloring books should not be confused with art education, I don't believe having some around the house will destroy a child's creativity. An online interview with Mark Evans, an artist who deals in fantasy and science fiction illustration, supports this view. (Go to www.cloudmover. net/interview.htm.)

For our coloring book, each student is going to draw a picture or design using contour lines. Everyone will get a piece of 8½″ by 11″ computer paper, which they may turn in either direction. With a pencil, they should draw a picture or design using only outlines. Remind them not to fill in anything. They may leave negative space, like sky, but most of the picture should be shapes, because you can't color in a line. When you are satisfied with a student's composition, have them go over the lines with black marker. Encourage them to keep their lines even. Find a nice negative space in each picture for the pupil to put his or her name, also in black marker.

Collect all the pictures, orient them properly, and run enough copies for each student. I print them front and back and staple them in the corner. I also create a cover sheet that gives the year. Since this project comes late in the spring, I hand them out in time for students to take them home over the summer.

This project could be adapted for older students in several ways. They could do essentially the same lesson, perhaps centering around a theme or using observational contour drawings. Or they could make group or individual coloring books for young children. Perhaps the drawings could relate to something in science or history class and require some research, like detailed drawings of leaves or dinosaurs.

Every child must complete a drawing. I am fortunate that the classroom teachers are willing to allow stragglers to finish their marker lines during the course of their regular day. If you cannot work this out, you might need to provide some extra time.

Lesson 37: Calligraphic Lines and Symmetry

Lesson Summary: Students will create images by pulling paint-soaked string through folded paper.

Purpose: Students will learn about calligraphic lines and review symmetry.

Materials: 9″ × 12″ white construction paper, red, yellow, and blue tempera paint watered down slightly, shallow containers, kite string, pencils, paper towels

Review: Line (definition), contour, symmetry, primary colors, movement

New Vocabulary/Concept: Calligraphic line

Time: One period

Possible Visual Aids: The works of Mark Toby, examples of calligraphy

For this project, you will need kite string and watered-down tempera paint. Place three shallow containers on each table, each one holding a different primary color of tempera paint that has been watered down to a rich, inky consistency. You will have to experiment to achieve just the right thickness—you don't want it too watery. Drape a two-foot piece of kite string in each container, making sure that a few inches of one end hangs outside the paint. Put out paper towels as well.

After your review, explain that, unlike contour lines, some lines get thicker and thinner. Ask if anyone knows what "calligraphy" is. Calligraphy is the art of beautiful writing, and it frequently requires special tools, like flat-edged brushes or pens. If you can demonstrate this kind of line with a special marker or brush, that would be great. Or bring in some examples of calligraphy in a greeting card or from the Internet. I approximate it on the board by using the side of my marker. Discuss how lively such lines are. Explain that they are going to create similar lines in a very special way.

Have each child select a partner. If older students do this, a partner is still a good idea, but if a pupil does it alone, a fairly large, heavy book might come in handy. With an uneven number of smaller children, you could have a group of three or partner the odd child yourself. Explain that they are going to take turns being the "artist" and the "partner." For demonstration purposes, ask a student to be your partner and explain that you are the artist. (Be sure you have practiced a lot yourself.)

Fold a piece of 9″ by 12″ white construction paper in half, hamburger style. After placing your name on the outside of the book, open the paper and place it with the inside facing up. Starting with the yellow paint, pick the string up by the clean end and hold it over the container. Then, pinching the place where the paint starts lightly between thumb and forefinger of the other hand, pull up on the string, keeping your hands over the container. This strips off excess paint. (Don't pinch too tightly or you will remove too much paint and the project will not work well.) Briefly wipe your two fingers on a paper towel, then lay the painted part of the string over one half of the paper in an interesting swirl pattern, leaving the clean end hanging off the edge of the paper. Close the paper, and have your partner press down firmly on top with both hands, fingers splayed, while you pull the string out. The pressure should be strong enough to offer some resistance, but not so strong as to prevent the pull. It should make a noise. (An older child or adult doing this project alone can press down with a book.) You should pull straight out, not up. Place the yellow string back in its paint, open the paper, and repeat the process with the red paint and then again with the blue. (This order will prevent the colors from ruining the paints and muddying the strings.) Wonderful symmetrical patterns result from this procedure, as well as lively calligraphic lines that display a great deal of movement. Be sure to hold up your demonstration piece

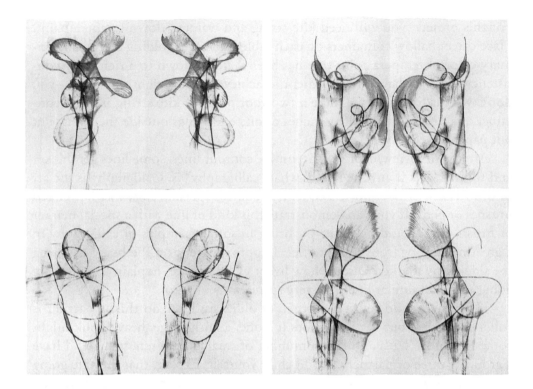

and ask if anyone knows what we call this type of design. They encountered symmetry in Lesson 5, and it might have been discussed in math class.

After your demonstration, the children simply take turns being artist and partner until time runs out. I pass out the first piece to avoid a traffic jam, then I place the paper and pencils in an easily accessible place, away from the messy tables. In a half-hour class, there is usually enough time for each student to do the procedure twice (four per team).

I use this process when we study line quality in first grade, but virtually any age student will enjoy it or one of its variations. You can probably imagine several versions of this project. One interesting twist involves using only black ink or paint and then trying to find a recognizable image in the result. Once the student finds such an image, he or she can enhance it with black marker.

Lesson 38: Still Life

Lesson Summary: Children will do observational drawings using pencil and paper.

Purpose: Children will use line to create artworks.

Materials: 12″ × 18″ white drawing or construction paper, pencils, subject matter if necessary, drawing boards (optional), black markers (optional)

Review: Line (definition), contour, calligraphic

New Vocabulary/Concepts: Observation, detail

Time: One or two periods

Possible Visual Aids: Works by Albrecht Durer

One of the best subjects for this lesson is potted plants, but virtually anything works, from art supplies, to the tables and chairs in the room, to each other. If conditions allow, you could take the students outdoors. This is, quite simply, observational drawing. My middle school students learn about "blind" contour drawing—that is, making line drawings where you don't look at your paper, but merely follow the edges of your subject. If you are working with older children, you might try that, using fine line black felt-tip pens or rollerball pens.

Review the usual material. Discuss the term "observation," and what it really means to "see." Elaborate as much as necessary, but make sure most of the period is used for work. Then simply point out the subject, give the students pencil and paper, and ask them to draw it in as much detail as possible. Encourage the children to "draw what they see, not what they know," to really look at what they are drawing. During the next period, you might go over the pencil lines with black marker for added drama.

Lesson 39:   File and Free

See Lesson 13.

Unit Six: **Form**

A three-dimensional, closed figure

Because form is so closely related to shape, you have already laid a lot of the groundwork for the introduction of this element. Sculpture and architecture examples are obvious choices for visual aids, although perspective and shading allow artists to create the illusion of form in paintings and drawings as well.

With the possible exception of the paper bag puppet, the students cannot put these projects in their portfolios, so they may take them at the end of each period. Thus, there is no "file and free" lesson included in this unit, but you may certainly add one if it works for you.

Lesson 40:   **Introduction to Form**

Lesson Summary: Students will be introduced to the concept of form and create a versatile paper figure.

Purpose: Students will learn the definition of form and create a form to reinforce the concept.

Materials: One 9″ × 12″ piece of construction paper (for demonstration), one pencil (for demonstration), various forms (optional), 12″ × 18″ construction paper, scissors, stapler

Review: Previously learned elements, shape (definition), dimension, geometric, organic, irregular

New Vocabulary/Concept: Form and its definition

Time: One period

Possible Visual Aids: Sculpture and architecture

Depending on the age level or math skills of your students, you might want to have some actual forms on hand—a ball, a shoe box, a cube of some sort, a cylindrical can, and a cone. You will know best what your children can conceptualize.

Begin by asking the students what elements they have already studied. After listing these on the board, ask what element is left, and write "form" as well. Ask the students what element already listed is the closest to form. Most should respond "shape." Review the definition of shape: a two-dimensional, closed figure. Ask if anyone can think what the definition of form might be. Someone should offer the information that forms are three-dimensional. Review the concept of dimensions and ask what dimension a form has that a shape does not. Write "thickness" and "depth" on the board. You might repeat the example from Lesson 27 about tracing someone versus sculpting them. "If you can pick something up, or if it casts a shadow, it is a form. One of the differences between a shape and a form is that a form can bear weight. Here's a magic trick you can show people." Hold up a piece of paper and a pencil. Construction paper works best for this. Hold the paper vertically so that one of its edges rests on a desk, and try to balance the pencil on the top edge. Of course it will always fall off. "How can I make this pencil balance on the edge of the paper without using any tape or glue or cutting anything?" Depending on the age of your students, you will get a variety of answers, but someone will probably get the general idea. Fold the paper in half and place it on the table. Place the pencil across the top of the "v" you have created. Everything will stand on its own. "I could not rest my pencil on a true triangle, but by making sort of a triangular prism, a form, I can support it.

"When we studied shape, we talked about different kinds of shapes. What did we call the shapes with names and rules? That's right, geometric. Well, there are geometric forms as well." Draw a circle on the board. "A circle is flat. What do we call a round object I can pick up?" Many small children will say "ball," but depending on the level of their math classes, some will know "sphere" as well. If not, you can introduce it. Next to the drawing of the circle, write "sphere." If it helps, use a real sphere, like a ball, to reinforce the concept. Repeat the process for several more forms. Draw a square on the board. Ask what we call a three-dimensional object with square sides. Write "cube" next to the square figure, and so forth. My class discusses spheres, cubes, cones, cylinders (a combination of circles and a rectangle), pyramids (triangles and a square), rectangular prisms (squares and rectangles), and triangular prisms (triangles and rectangles). If you are dealing with older students, they may suggest others. You can also discuss organic forms, like people or trees, and irregular forms, like airplanes or cars. Explain that we can repeat and relate forms the same way we can shapes.

"As we discussed in our unit on shape, a piece of paper is technically a form, but artists refer to it as a two-dimensional medium when they use it to paint or draw, because they are not concerned with the edges or back. We are going to do several projects in which we create three-dimensional forms from these flat pieces of paper."

Give each student a piece of 12″ by 18″ construction paper. I prefer white for this exercise, but any color will work, so each child might choose something different. You need not worry about names, because students will take these home right away and they will all be alike. This is one of those rare occasions when we are not focusing on creativity or uniqueness, although you will offer them suggestions for using this form in personal ways. The purpose here is simply to reinforce the concept of form in a fun way. Also, rather than doing a demonstration first, have them do each step as you do it, and check their accuracy as you go.

Fold the paper in a hot dog fold. Open the paper and, valley side facing you, fold one of the long edges to the center fold and press down. Repeat this process on the other side of the original fold. This should yield three parallel folds that evenly divide the paper longwise into four sections, with all the mountains on the same side of the page.

Open the paper and fold it along the original center fold. Hold it so that the fold is on the bottom, and pick up a pair of scissors. Remind the students of the looms they made for their weaving project. This will be very similar. About an inch (or a little less) in from one edge, cut straight up from the bottom fold until you reach the next fold. Cut very slightly beyond that fold. Move over about the same distance away from the first cut and repeat the process. Continue until you reach the other end of the paper.

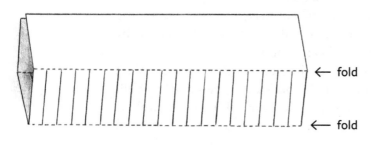

Nothing should fall off, and the cuts shouldn't be too far apart or too close together. Open the paper and make sure the cuts reach the folds on both sides of the page. Fold the paper back along the center fold and cut off a single fringe from one end of your paper. Either end is fine. When most of the students have caught up, show them how to create the form. Open the paper. Overlap the two solid sides to create a triangular prism with one solid side and two slitted ones.

There should be a tab at one end, where you cut off the piece of fringe. Show how flexible this form is. Hold it at each end and arch it. (If it doesn't flow eas-

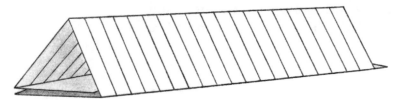

ily, check your cuts to make sure they reach the folds.) You can twist it and make it go up and down like a slinky. Suggest all the different things students could do with this form. They could put two different colors of paper together before making it, so that the inside contrasts with the outside. They could put several forms together, or curve them into a circle. Show them how to do this. Bring the two ends together and staple the tab securely into the opposite end to complete the form. The result can be used in a number of ways. They look like tires on a truck, crowns, suns, and flowers. They could be stacked to make sculptures. For older students, this exercise could be the lead-in to a broader lesson on paper sculpture, or they could be challenged to create an artwork based on this form.

Lesson 41: The Captain's Shirt

Lesson Summary: Children will listen to the story of "The Captain's Shirt" and learn to fold the various illustrations.

Purpose: This project will reinforce the concept of form and teach some basic origami.

Materials: Newspaper or manila paper

Review: Element, form (definition), geometric, irregular

New Vocabulary/Concept: Origami

Time: One period

Possible Visual Aids: Origami examples or books

This lesson and the next involve stories illustrated during the telling with origami. Depending upon the age of your students and the general curriculum, you might want to relate this lesson to Japanese culture or explore origami in more depth. Perhaps your students have read *Sadako and the Thousand Cranes* by Eleanor Coerr. Or you might skip these two lessons entirely and do a ceramics unit instead. (See Lesson 43.) For my first graders, I use the stories and folding techniques simply to reinforce the concept of form, without a great deal of background. Origami is a wonderful and inexpensive way to create three-dimensional figures. As an added benefit, it demonstrates the importance of following instructions carefully. This exercise also uses several very basic and useful folds.

I learned "The Captain's Shirt" many years ago from the young daughter of a friend. It is a classic that appears in a wide variety of forms in origami books and on the Internet. As I learned it, the story concerns a young boy who likes to walk on the beach and daydream about what he wants to be when he grows up. He thinks he might like to be a sea captain, and the first folded form is a captain's hat. But he changes his mind and decides to be a fireman, so the captain's hat becomes a fireman's hat (the second form). His third choice is to become Robin Hood, whose hat is the third form. While he is thinking about that, he sees a sailboat in the distance (the fourth form). While he's watching it, a terrible storm comes up, and the boat breaks apart, losing its prow, its stern, and part of the sail. (These are ripped off.) The boy runs to get help, but as the narrator unfolds the form that is left, she explains that all that they find floating on the water is the captain's shirt. (I usually add that the captain was found alive and well on an island a couple of days later.) Most of the versions on the Internet are abbreviated, but some have wonderful illustrations. Go to http://rachel.ns.purchase.edu/–Jeanine/origami/oriexam.htm for particularly nice animated instructions. Or simply type "captain's shirt origami" into your Web browser and find a site or book that works for you.

Start the class with a very brief review, simply asking what element you are exploring and its definition. You might also review the nature of geometric forms. Ask if anyone knows what origami is, and define it. (I simply say it is the Japanese art of folding paper into wonderful forms. My students usually are familiar with it, so I need not spend a great deal of time describing it, but you might want to have some examples on hand.) Then explain that you are going to tell them a special story. (Of course, when I tell it, I add a lot of detail. For instance, after demonstrating the fireman's hat, I ask why such hats have a longer brim in the back. When I come to the part about the storm, I turn on one of my faucets, hold my hand under the water, and fling "rain-drops" over everyone.)

After the story is over, take the students step by step through the various folds. You might pause after each step and ask if the resulting form is geometric or irregular.

Making the boat is the most difficult part, and you might want to help students individually "pull" the paper into this form. I let my students decide if they want to tear the boat to make the shirt or leave it alone. Such paper boats will float for a while. I don't bother with names. Once again, this is not a creative project, and the students may take the results with them.

Lesson 42:   The Story of "Paper Flower"

Lesson Summary: Children will learn to fold one or more of the forms from the story "Paper Flower," by Fran Stallings.

Purpose: The lesson will reinforce the concepts of form and origami.

Materials: Construction paper, tissue paper, or newsprint (optional for flower), scissors, paper lantern (optional)

Review: Element, form (definition), origami

New Vocabulary/Concepts: Lantern, fanfold

Time: One period

"Paper Flower" is another delightful story illustrated with paper forms. It was written by Fran Stallings and tells the story of a poor Chinese farm girl who goes to the big city to earn money for her family. She promises to work for a very mean lady for one year if, at the end of that time, she can go home for a visit. The mean lady tries to trick her into staying, but using some very clever paper folding, the young girl wins her freedom and becomes a successful businesswoman. The entire story, with necessary instructions, appears in *Joining In: An Anthology of Audience Participation Stories and How to Tell Them*, available from Yellow Moon Press. The folds include a paper cup, a fan, a lantern, and a flower. Of course, you will want to dramatize it as much as possible, filling the cup with real water (be sure to use paper that doesn't leak) and shaking the fan in students' faces. You might want to start the lantern, to show the students how it is made, but have a finished one (with a bottom and handle) set aside to save time.

After a brief review and sharing the story with your students, you have several options for a culminating activity. Depending on your time frame, you might have the students fold any or all of the aforementioned forms. If you choose the paper cup, don't precut the paper into squares. Show the children how to create a square from a rectangle by folding the short edge down along the long edge and cutting or tearing the excess paper. This is a very helpful skill and has nice math implications. If you want to add a more creative element, and time is not an issue, have the students decorate both sides of a piece of paper and fanfold it. This project and the previous one would work nicely into a unit on Asian cultures.

Lesson 43: Working with Clay

Lesson Summary: Children will mold forms from clay.

Purpose: Children will learn how to create organic forms from clay.

Materials: Clay or other malleable material, old sheets or newspapers (optional)

Review: Element, form (with definition), organic clay tools or craft sticks (optional)

New Vocabulary/Concepts: Sculpture, clay, molding

Time: One period

Possible Visual Aid: Sculpture by Henry Moore

This is a very simple project. After your review, simply pass out small chunks of clay and let the students sculpt freely. You might want to cover your tables with old sheets, or let each child work on a piece of newspaper, but desktops are fine as well. I prefer Triarco brand self-hardening clay, which is very inexpensive and does not require a kiln, but you have several alternatives. If time is not a factor and your school has a kiln, you might use regular clay and fire the students' works. Depending on your budget and expertise, you might even allow the children to glaze them as well. On the other hand, if your budget is tight, you could make one of the several recipes for Play-Doh-like materials that appear in books or on the Web. Here is one:

Place one cup salt, two cups plain flour, two cups water, two tablespoons cooking oil, and four teaspoons cream of tartar in a pan and heat gently until it forms a lump and leaves the sides of the pan. Allow to cool thoroughly and store in an airtight container.

Whatever material you use should be malleable for the length of the period. If you have clay tools or craft sticks you might put them out as well. The forms the children create will probably be organic, so you might want to discuss this as they work. Simply allow the students to mold freely and take their projects with them.

Of course, for older children, a ceramics unit would serve as a great vehicle for the discussion of form.

Lesson 44:   Paper Bag Puppets

Lesson Summary: Children will create puppets out of small paper bags.

Purpose: The project will reinforce the concept of form and allow the students to use form creatively.

Materials: Brown paper lunch bags, crayons and/or markers, construction paper in assorted colors (optional), yarn and/or fabric (optional), glue sticks (optional), stapler (optional)

Review: Form, dimension, depth

New Vocabulary/Concepts: Puppet, front, back, sides

Time: One or two periods

Possible Visual Aids: Famous puppets, perhaps from *Sesame Street*, discussed as sculpture

I rarely have time for this project, but it is fun for small children and a nice way to reinforce the concept of form. You will need a small brown lunch bag for each child. A local store might be willing to donate these. You can do this with crayons or markers only, or you can put out colored paper, scissors, and glue sticks to create added details.

After your review, show the children a flattened (rectangular) lunch bag. Turn it so that the opening is at the bottom and the flap is facing up, and slide your hand inside, palm side up. Curve your fingers into the bottom flap and show the students how the bag can talk like a puppet. Once you have established where the mouth is, you can draw one on your bag and add some eyes. Do just enough of a demonstration that the children can get the idea, then let them create their own characters. If you need ideas, you can go to any of a myriad Internet sites, but please don't use patterns or handouts for this project. Students can use extra paper, fabric, or yarn to create limbs, ears, tails, and so forth. (Or simply draw these features on.) You might want to staple cutouts on instead of gluing. The important point to stress is that the puppet is a form, and that, therefore, *all four sides must be considered*. They cannot just draw on the front and call it a day. Unlike a two-dimensional artwork, such as a painting or a drawing, a sculpture, or three-dimensional work, can be viewed from all sides, so they must make all the sides special. If they see a dog or cat or friend from the sides or back, that view isn't blank.

This project offers many possibilities for integration. The characters could illustrate a unit being taught in the regular classroom or a story written by the students themselves. Or it could inspire a student to write a story. The children could create a zoo or a jungle population or aliens from another planet. The puppet could be a self-portrait. This project allows even the oldest students a chance to express themselves in a fun and creative way. Fandango, a company that allows people to buy movie tickets in advance, uses paper bag puppets in their advertisements, so many children will be familiar with the concept.

Lesson 45: Contrast and Compare Two Artworks

Lesson Summary: The children will contrast and compare two artworks.

Purpose: Students will see how artists use the elements of art to achieve their purpose.

Materials: Two artworks, real or reproductions

Review: (In the course of the discussion) element, color, shape, texture, value, line, form, illusion (many others, depending on the images)

New Vocabulary/Concepts: Contrast, compare

Time: One period

Suggested Visual Aids: *Sunday Afternoon on the Island of La Grande Jatte*, by Georges Seurat; and *Paris Street; Rainy Day*, by Gustave Caillebotte

The last class of each of the first three years is devoted to the same activity—looking at art. In this instance, you are going to select two artworks. You can choose virtually any images for this, but for younger children at least, I recommend narrative paintings—that is, relatively realistic images that tell a story. My favorite choices for this first experience are Georges Seurat's *Sunday Afternoon on the Island of La Grande Jatte* and *Paris Street; Rainy Day* by Gustave Caillebotte. Both paintings are in the collection of the Art Institute of Chicago, and you can get wonderful posters of the pieces from the museum or online. Whatever images you choose, you will need to create a situation where they can be seen clearly by all the students. If you use images printed off the Internet, you might want to make several copies. Of course, the best experience would involve real artworks, but the pieces need to be close enough to be easily compared.

One of the best ways of getting people to really look at an artwork is an exercise called "Generating a Word List." This process is explained on pages 100–101 of *Art Matters*, and it can be done with even the youngest children. If time allows, you could use one or both of the images for that exercise before having the students contrast and compare.

Ask the class if anyone knows what "contrast" (as a verb) means, and elicit a definition that involves "finding things that are different between two or more items." Repeat the process for the word "compare," and help the students understand that when we compare things, we are frequently looking for features they have in common—features that are similar or the same. So if they contrast and compare two artworks, that means they are going to find things that are alike and different about them. Make sure that everyone can see the images you have chosen, then simply ask leading questions and allow the children to discuss the pieces. Some possible questions might be: What elements did the artists use? (Encourage them to elaborate on each of these. How did this artist use texture? What colors do you see? Did the artists use real form or illusion?) What things do you see that are alike in the two images? What things are different? What do you think the artist was trying to show us in this painting? How did he use art elements to do that? Contrasting and comparing artworks will help children focus on the pieces and look at them closely. You might be surprised at the perceptive observations they will make.

Second Year

THE SECOND YEAR of the curriculum generally includes lessons that reinforce and expand upon the concepts covered in year one. The projects and reviews usually include some new idea or vocabulary word, so please read through them carefully before omitting anything.

Lesson 1: Creating a Portfolio

See First Year, Lesson 1. Depending upon the age and maturity of your students, of course, you will adjust the rules and instructions.

Unit One: **Color**

Lesson 2:   **Reviewing Color Theory**

Lesson Summary: Students will review the color and value concepts and vocabulary learned in year one, stressing the importance of light.

Purpose: The review will help returning students recall and remember vocabulary and concepts. New students will be introduced to color and value terms and concepts, and all children will observe the importance of light to color.

Materials: Paint used to demonstrate color mixing (the primaries of tempera work well), water, brushes, and paper for demo, a projector screen or large white surface, like a wall, a light source (such as a projector or strong flashlight), colored plastic (report covers or gels used in theatrical lighting)

Review: Light, how we see color, white, black, gray, rainbow, primary, why primaries are important, secondaries, intermediates, tertiaries, complementary colors, value

New Vocabulary/Concepts: Hue, the effect of light on color

Time: Two periods

I spend the first two periods of the second year reviewing the color and value vocabulary and concepts we learned in first grade and stressing the importance of light. If there are new students, they get to go into the dark room (see First Year, Lesson 14), and everyone looks through the rainbow glasses. We discuss white light and the nature of black, and we introduce a new term for color: hue. Hue refers to the name of a color. Red is a different hue than red-orange. We review the primaries, why they are important, and how they can be combined to form secondaries, intermediates, and even tertiaries. (See the first-year unit on color.) We briefly cover complementary colors and how they can brighten or dull each other, but I don't spend much time on this, because we will be going over it in greater detail later in the unit. The review is in a question and answer format, and the material is accompanied by a demonstration using paint. This discussion is very helpful to students who covered the concepts in first grade, as well as to those who have just joined the class. While the review is somewhat brief, the concepts will be reinforced in the first two projects.

One of the ideas I stress during this review is the importance of light to color. Because the color is in the light, the quality of the light is vital to what we see. There is an easy way to demonstrate this concept, and I think even older students would enjoy the experience.

You will need a projector of some sort, several colored pieces of plastic (essay covers work well, but gels used in theatrical lighting would be terrific), and a white surface. I have used old filmstrip projectors, but even a strong flashlight should work. Darken the room as much as possible. Aim the light at the white surface and ask the students what they see. Review why they see white, and elicit the response that all the light is bouncing off the surface. Now place a piece of red plastic in front of the light and ask what they see. Why is the surface red? It is still reflecting back all the light, but the only light hitting it is red. Now have someone stand in front of the light, preferably someone wearing a bright shirt. If the shirt is green, you can turn it gray or black by using the red plastic. If it is yellow, it will look orangey. Have different students stand in front of the light, and use mostly red, blue, and green plastics. (The yellow is too wimpy to cause a noticeable reaction.) The colors on their clothing will change drastically as you change the color of the light.

After this demonstration and a brief discussion of the light in artists' studios, I tell the following true story to demonstrate why light is so important when using color. Perhaps you have had a similar experience you can share with your students.

As a wedding gift, someone gave us a bedspread in the (then) popular color of avocado green. I decided to make some curtains to go with the spread. I took it to a fabric store and selected some cloth that matched perfectly under the fluorescent lights in the shop and in the daylight. When I got home, I made the (very simple) drapes and put them up. My husband arrived home after dark, so when I took him into the bedroom to see the new curtains, I turned on the incandescent light next to the bed. Lo and behold, my drapes were a muddy brown! In order to appear green, the dye needed some wavelength that was missing from incandescent light. The dye used on the spread, on the other hand, reflected a combination of wavelengths that my brain read as green. It is very important to match colors in the light they will be seen in. Someone picking carpet or wallpaper or upholstery, or matching a sweater to a pair of slacks, needs to be sure to look at them in daylight and in the kind of lamplight or office light that will be used to light them. Greens are particularly susceptible to change.

Lesson 3:   Mixing Primaries

Lesson Summary: Students will create an informally tessellated design of shapes using black marker, then fill it in using and mixing red, yellow, and blue crayons.

Purpose: Students will see how primaries mix to form secondaries, intermediates, tertiaries, browns, and values.

Materials: 12″ × 18″ white construction paper, pencils, black markers, red, yellow, and blue crayons

Review: Tessellation, primary colors (definition), secondary, intermediate, tertiary, value

Time: Five or six periods

Possible Visual Aids: Works by Georges Seurat, showing how the pointillist dots of pure color combine to form a huge variety of secondaries, intermediates, and tertiaries

This lesson serves as a strong reinforcement of color concepts learned in year one. While older students could do variations using other media, like oil pastel or paint, I urge you to have them do it as written. The lowly crayon is often overlooked as a medium in the upper grades, but I think you will have new respect for its possibilities once you have seen the results of this project.

Start with a review of the primary colors and why they are important. The rest of the review can occur as you proceed with the demonstration. Show the class a piece of 9″ by 12″ white construction paper and explain that they will be using one for this lesson, and they can turn it in either direction. Draw a larger rectangle on the board so that everyone can see your work. Explain that there will be three steps to this project. The first step is to create a picture or design in pencil that tessellates the page. (See First Year, Lesson 22 for a discussion of tessellation. You will probably need to review this concept.) They must use their pencils very lightly, and they should not make any tiny shapes. When you have OKed this step, they will be allowed to go over their pencil lines carefully with black marker. Draw an appropriate design or picture on your large rectangle so that they can get the idea.

Place a piece of white paper on the board and draw some shapes on it in black marker. Explain to the class that they are only going to use three crayons to fill in the entire page. What three colors do they think these will be? Right—the primary colors! Does this mean that the entire page will be red, yellow, and blue? Of course not. In fact, the color possibilities are practically unlimited, because the primaries can be mixed to form every other color.

Color one of the shapes on the paper red, and explain that they may use a primary by itself, but that when you look at the finished project, you want to see mostly secondaries and intermediates. Put a fairly heavy layer of yellow in another shape and color over it with red until you have created a relatively medium orange. Ask what kind of color orange is, and elicit the response "secondary." Briefly define secondary, then ask how one makes an intermediate. When a student responds that you mix two primaries unevenly, use a new space to demonstrate the result. Repeat the process you used to create the orange, but add very little red to create a yellow-orange, and in yet another shape, mix more red to make a red-orange. In a good-sized shape, lay down a layer of one color, using gradation to go from one value to another, then reverse the gradation when you apply the second color. Thus the shape might gradually go from red-orange through orange to yellow-orange. Show the class that there are many different red-oranges and yellow-oranges. Demonstrate that different effects are achieved by using the crayon heavily versus using it lightly.

Review the concept of tertiary colors and ask the students how they might create a tertiary using the three primaries. Technically, they could mix two primaries to make a secondary, then mix a different pair right on top. Many if not most of the sections that are filled with all three colors will be a tertiary of some sort. These are great fun, but remind the students that the goal is to create mostly secondaries and intermediates. If all three colors are mixed somewhat evenly, the children will get a brownish tone, while some unequal mixes can produce a gray or black. (If they mix blue and yellow to make green and add just the right amount of its complement, red.)

Second grader John Moore used only three primary-colored crayons to create this project. (See color insert)

All of the shapes will be filled in. None will be left white. If a student is upset that his cloud or sheep cannot be white, explain that he can use a primary very lightly and that most white things really aren't if we observe them closely. Also, when students are ready to use crayons, remind them to check the label to make sure they have selected true red, true yellow, and true blue.

Lesson 4: Color Mixing with Watercolors—Intermediates and Tertiaries

Lesson Summary: Students will mix hues and values using watercolors.

Purpose: Students will explore new ways to create intermediates and compare the effects of mixed versus straight secondaries; they will also review good painting technique.

Materials: 12″ × 18″ white construction paper, crayons, watercolors (regular eight-color box with brush), water buckets, paper towels, pencils (optional, except for names)

Review: Primary (define, why they are important), secondary (way to mix), intermediate (way to mix), tertiary (way to mix), value (way to mix), brown (way to mix)

New Vocabulary/Concepts: Mixing an intermediate from a primary and a related, or non-opposite, secondary

Time: Six to eight periods

Possible Visual Aid: Marc Franz, *Deer in Forest I*

This lesson is essentially a variation on the previous one. Since the review and demonstration will take some time, you might not begin the project until the next period. You will not need watercolor set up until students have completed the crayon stage of the process. Then you will need paint buckets, paper towels, and watercolors.

Briefly review the color theory covered in Lesson 3. Then place a 12″ by 18″ piece of white construction paper on the board. Explain to the students that they are going to create a similar type of design as in the last project. That is, they are going to tessellate the page, only this time their lines are going to be made with heavy, waxy crayon. I prefer my students to work directly with crayon, but if you allow the students to start with pencil, the pencil lines must be very light. You might have the children go over them with art gum erasers before adding the crayon. This project uses a process known as crayon resist, so it is imperative that the crayon lines be solid and waxy. If properly done, the wax used as the crayon's binder will resist the watercolor painted over it and show through. If the crayon is not waxy enough, the paint will simply cover it. If you can see the texture of the paper through the crayon, it is probably too thin. The lines should be tidy, not shaggy or sketchy, and the students may use any crayons they wish. They might use one crayon for all the lines or every color in the box. Remind them that if they use white, it must be balanced around the paper. Demonstrate by drawing a few shapes on your paper. Shapes may overlap to create the design, but none of the shapes should be too big or too small.

The next step involves the watercolor. Review the proper use of a brush from First Year, Lesson 6. A normal box of school watercolors has eight patties: red, yellow, blue, orange, green, violet, brown, and black. They may use any of these except the brown or black, and they must mix. Therefore, a project should demonstrate a wide variety of colors. They could include primary colors, which can only be achieved by using a color straight out of the box. A secondary color could also be taken straight out of the box or created by mixing two primaries. On your demonstration paper, paint a secondary, such as orange, and then in another place on the page mix the same secondary by using its two primaries, in this case red and yellow. In the first project, there was only one way to make a secondary or an intermediate—by mixing two primaries evenly or unevenly. Now they have options. An intermediate can still be made by mixing two primaries unevenly, but it can also be made by mixing a primary with a related, or non-opposite, secondary. You can demonstrate by filling a shape with unequal amounts of red and yellow to create a yellow-orange and then matching that intermediate by using yellow and orange. Discuss the logic of this. Tertiaries will be much easier to create because you can mix secondaries directly. Demonstrate the three tertiaries on your paper. Mixing opposites will result in tones approaching gray or black.

Aside from the medium, there will be another big difference between this project and the last. The crayon mix project looks much better if the students stay inside the lines. In this project, you are going to require them to paint outside the lines. This should be done in a controlled way, just going slightly over the lines. This will ensure that there is a great deal of color mixing, even if the student doesn't mix frequently inside the shapes.

Second graders Meena Moorthy and Anne Havlik created these terrific projects. (See color insert)

Lesson 5:   File and Free

If time allows, you might insert a "file and free" period here (see First Year, Lesson 13). If not, simply move ahead to Lesson 6.

Lesson 6:   Introduction to Color Schemes

Lesson Summary: Students will create a picture or design that will serve as the basis for the study of color schemes.

Purpose: Students will be introduced to the general concept of color schemes.

Materials: 12″ × 18″ white construction paper, pencils, crayons, access to a paper cutter or an X-Acto knife

Review: Color, primary, secondary

New Vocabulary/Concepts: scheme (general definition), color scheme

Time: Two to three periods

Although I will offer suggestions for visual aids for each color scheme lesson, you might approach this a little differently. After reading through the next four lessons, you might look at Claude Monet's series of wheat stack paintings or views of Rouen Cathedral and select several with different color schemes. The study of color schemes is more powerful if you can see the effect of different schemes on the same subject.

After asking what element of art they have been studying (color), explain that the next several lessons will explore color schemes. Ask if anyone knows what "scheme" means. Write the word on the board, and elicit the information that it means "a plot or a plan." You can elaborate on this, but focus on the word "plan." A color scheme is a plan of colors that an artist intends to use in an artwork. Ask the students, "When you draw a picture, how many of you pick certain colors when you begin? How many just use crayons or markers randomly as you go along? How many do some pictures one way and some the other? Artists work this way as well. Sometimes artists have a plan of colors before they begin. They might choose those particular colors for a variety of reasons. Perhaps they want to tie everything together. Perhaps they want to attract attention. Maybe the colors are natural to the subject—many landscapes have related colors of grass, trees, and sky. Certain combinations of colors work well together, and have been used by artists through the centuries. We are going to study four of these traditional combinations, and we are going to do it in a somewhat unusual way."

Explain that each of them will start with a piece of 12″ by 18″ white construction paper that they may turn in either direction. Before they begin, the children must place their names on the back in a special way. After deciding which way to orient the page, they should place their name on the back in each of the four corners, followed by the number of the corner.

Then, using a pencil, they are going to draw an interesting picture or design lightly on the front of the page. They do not need to tessellate the paper. They are welcome to leave a background, but as in all projects, the image must be well composed, and interesting shapes should appear evenly around the page. When you have OKed their picture, they are to select a primary or secondary color and go over all the lines carefully. They should double check the color name of their crayon to make sure it is a true primary or secondary. Stress the fact that the pencil lines must be very light. If they seem too dark, have the student lighten them with an art gum eraser before adding the crayon. Emphasize good craftsmanship (as always). In this case, that means staying on the lines and not making them sketchy or too wide. They need not be waxy, but they should be strong and clear. These lines could also be done with marker.

Explain that when they have covered all their lines with crayon, you are going to slice their pictures into four parts. They should not let this fact influence their design. This project will be far more interesting if the cuts go through parts of their picture, like houses or dogs or just shapes, than if they make a design in quadrants. When OKing a composition, check the four quarters of the design to make sure each has several interesting shapes. Each one of the quarters will be colored in a different color scheme, then the pieces will be put back together. We spend about two periods drawing and coloring the basic design lines before we begin discussing the actual color schemes. A student who is not finished may continue covering lines when the rest start coloring the first scheme. When all the lines are covered in crayon, I use a paper cutter to divide the paper in half each way, yielding four 6″ by 9″ pieces. (An X-Acto knife would work as well.)

A variation on this project would involve creating four identical compositions, either by tracing or using a copy machine. If you use a machine, set it to

Second grader John Khantsis's anteater is split into four different color schemes. (See color insert)

copy very lightly, then add the crayon. Older students might use paint rather than the media suggested in the next lessons.

Lesson 7: Monochromatic Color Schemes

Lesson Summary: Students will color one of the sections from the previous lesson using a monochromatic color scheme.

Purpose: Students will learn the definition of a monochromatic color scheme and observe its effect.

Materials: 6″ × 9″ section from previous lesson, colored pencils, crayons, markers

Review: Value, tint, shade, hue, primary, secondary

New Vocabulary/Concepts: Monochromatic, three properties of color, intensity, prefix "mono," words that begin with mono

Time: Three periods

Possible Visual Aids: Victor Vasarely, *Cheyt M*; Saiki Hoitsu, *Cranes*; Yoruba Peoples, *Adire Cloth* (blue)

For the next four lessons, I usually use one period to introduce the concept and then give the students two periods to color in a quarter. Older students using this format would not need as much time.

After reviewing the concept of color schemes, write the word "monochromatic" on the board and draw a line between "mono" and "chromatic." Ask if anyone knows what the prefix "mono" means. You might begin by asking if anyone can give you another word that begins with this prefix. I am fortunate that many of my students have been to a regional theme park that has a monorail, so I can lead them in that direction. They also love dinosaurs, so I frequently hear about a monoclonius or monoceratops. By the time we have listed two or three items, the students usually catch on to the idea that "mono" means "one."

List as many words as you can. I introduce and elicit such terms as monopoly, monocle (the Monopoly guy helps here), monotheism, monotone, monotonous, monoplane, monologue, monogram, monopolize, and monophonic. (This is a great time to invite your principal in to observe!) You might also have your students each bring in three words from the dictionary that begin with the prefix, or even make up funny terms that use it.

Once the students are comfortable with the meaning of "mono," underline "chroma" and explain that it comes from the Greek word for color. So how many colors are there in a monochromatic color scheme? That's right, one! Since everyone chose a color for their lines, that is the color they must use. You might ask, "But if I fill in all my purple lines with purple, or blue lines with blue, how will I see my shapes? What can I do to my color that will change it without changing the hue? Let's say that I chose red for my lines." (Write "red" on the board.) "What else could I use in my picture besides red, something that is not a color? Yes! I can always use black, white, and gray, because they are values, not colors." (Add black, white, and gray to the list.) "I can use black as black, but what else could I do with it? That's right, I can mix it with my red to make a darker value of my color. What do we call a color with black added? Exactly—a shade! Does anyone know what we call a shade of red?" (Elicit or supply the word "maroon," and add it to the list with the word "shade," because there are virtually limitless possibilities of darker values.) "I can use white as itself, but what else could I do with it? Of course, add it to my red! What do we call a color with white added? Great—a tint! What do we call a tint of red?" (Elicit or supply "pink," and add it and "tint" to your list.) "I can use gray as itself, but what else can I do with it? Let's say my gray is exactly the same value as my red. What happens to my red when I mix it with the gray?"

It is a good idea to stop here and elaborate on the concept of dull and bright. You might use something like the following example.

"There are three basic ways we define or describe a color. Let's say I painted my bedroom and I want you to picture it. What is the first, most obvious thing I would tell you? Of course, the name of the color! Did I choose blue or blue-green or yellow? If I tell you the room is blue, is that enough information for you to picture it exactly? How else might I describe the color? That's right, I could tell you how light or dark it is—its value! What is the third way I could describe the color?" If students have a problem here, look around the room for two children who are wearing different versions of the same color. One might have a Colts or Cowboys blue football jersey, and someone else might be wearing faded blue jeans. Ask the students to describe the difference, and persevere until somebody uses the terms "bright" and "dull." Point out that light is different than bright, and dark is different than dull. A color can be light and bright or light and dull. It can be dark and bright or dark and dull. Find examples in the class if possible. Explain that the brightness of a color depends on its purity. Artists refer to the brightness or dullness of a color as its "intensity." The three ways we define or describe a color are by its hue (name), value (lightness and darkness), and intensity (brightness and dullness).

Go back to the original question: what happens to a color if we add a gray of the same value? It gets duller. If we add gray to red, we get a dull red. If we add gray to pink, we call the result "rose." Add these words to your list. There are other ways to dull a color, but for this section, we are only going to use our base color, black, white, and gray. (If you are dealing with older children and using paint, you might allow them to dull a color by using its opposite—see complementary colors.)

The students may use colored pencils, crayons, and markers. This will give them more variety of pure colors. Caution them to stick to the primaries or secondaries that match their lines. Blue-green is not a form of blue—it is a different hue, an intermediate.

Have them select one of the quarters you cut in the previous lesson. Any one of the four will do—it need not be number one. They are to color the piece, using only the color they used for their lines, although they may adjust its value and/or intensity. They may use pure values as well, and any or all the suggested media. Caution them to stay carefully in the lines. This is like a puzzle, and it won't go back together correctly if the lines don't match.

Aside from exploring famous artworks, you could mention such careers as interior design and clothing design, where color schemes are vitally important. You may want to discuss why an artist might choose a monochromatic color scheme. Rooms and outfits, as well as paintings, can be unified by the use of a single color. Also, caution the students that the color scheme refers to the predominant color or colors. A little area of some other color does not change the whole scheme, but for our purposes, we will keep our sections pure.

Lesson 8:   Complementary Color Schemes

Lesson Summary: Students will fill in one of the sections from Lesson 6 using a complementary color scheme.

Purpose: Students will explore the nature and effect of complementary colors.

Materials: 6″ × 9″ section from Lesson 6, markers, colored pencils, crayons

Review: Complementary colors (definition), effect, side by side, mixing, value, simultaneous contrast

New Vocabulary/Concept: Complementaries as a color scheme

Time: Three periods

Possible Visual Aids: Frank Benson, *Sunlight*; Willard Leroy Metcalf, *October*; Jan Van Eyck, *Arnolfini and His Bride*

The second quarter of the project will be filled in with a complementary color scheme. The materials will be the same as for Lesson 7, and you will begin by reviewing the concept of color schemes and nature of monochromatic plans.

Explain that the second color scheme you are going to explore is already familiar to the class. Review what the students know about complementary colors: how they discovered complements, what the basic sets of complements are, what the word means, and so forth. (See First Year, Lessons 10, 11, and 12.) Hold up the circles and stare, and point out the location of complements on the color wheel. In short, your review should be both verbal and visual.

Focus especially on the effect complements have upon each other. Hold a piece of green paper next to a piece of red and have the students stare, just as you did in year one. Notice how the edges vibrate and the colors seem to intensify. Discuss the reason for this effect. You can create an even better demonstration of this effect, which you might remember is called simultaneous contrast. Start with a piece of 9″ by 12″ red construction paper. Cover one half of it with a 6″ by 9″ piece of yellow construction paper. (Glue this on.) Cut a circular hole with about a two-inch diameter in the center of each half. Place a piece of 9″ by 12″ green construction paper behind the whole thing. Show the results to your students in such a way that they only see two green circles, one against a red background and one against yellow. Ask them if the two green circles look exactly alike. After a few seconds, the circle surrounded by yellow should appear darker and duller than the one surrounded by red. Pull the green paper away and show the class that both circles actually were identical. Stress the fact that when opposite colors are placed side by side, they intensify each other. Artists might use complementary colors if they want to attract attention or make a picture glow.

Ask if anyone remembers what happens when complementary colors are mixed. Using paint, demonstrate the fact that when opposite colors are mixed unevenly, they dull each other. Place a large amount of green on a piece of paper and add a touch of red. I suggest red and green, because they are likely to be the closest to actual opposites. Lighten the result with water so that the students can see the dulling effect of the complement. If you mix more equal amounts, you should get gray or black.

Go over the basic pairs of opposites, making sure everyone knows that all colors have opposites, not just these few. Remind the class that complements lie directly across from each other on the color wheel. The review of basic pairs can be done in the form of a question and answer session. "If your lines are red, what will your two colors be? If your lines are yellow, what will your two colors be?" and so forth.

Explain that, once again, students may use the values as themselves or mix them with the colors to create tints and shades. They may also mix the two opposites to create a gray or very dark value. I ask my students to fill at least two adjoining shapes in pure opposites—a red right next to a green, for instance—and to mix opposites in at least one space. One thing you should stress in this and the next two lessons is that if they used pure black or white in their first quarter, they should be prepared to use that value in all the quarters, so that the project is balanced. Also, if a student uses white in only one section, it will seem as if the space simply wasn't colored in. They may use the same media as in Lesson 7.

Lesson 9: Triadic Color Schemes

Lesson Summary: Students will color one of the sections from Lesson 6 using a triadic color scheme.

Purpose: Students will learn the definitions and effect of a triadic color scheme.

Materials: 6″ × 9″ section from Lesson 6, colored pencils, markers, crayons

Review: Color scheme, monochromatic, complementary, value, intensity, tint, shade

New Vocabulary/Concepts: Triadic, equilateral triangle, prefix "tri," words that begin with tri

Time: Three periods

Possible Visual Aids: Works by Roy Lichtenstein, later works by Piet Mondrian, Claude Monet's *Villas a Bordighera*

Students will need the same materials as for the previous two lessons. This introduction will follow the same pattern as the introduction to monochromatic color schemes.

After reviewing the terms "color scheme," "monochromatic," and "complementary," write the word "triadic" on the board and mark off the prefix "tri." Ask if anyone knows what that prefix means, and create a word list of terms such as tricycle, triangle, triceratops, triplets, tribunal, and so forth. Ask who can guess how many colors are in a triadic color scheme. When someone answers "three," ask if they can think of a group of three special colors we have discussed before. Of course, they should respond "primaries." Then ask if there is another group of three colors that they can think of. When you have elicited the concept secondary, have the students find these colors on the class color wheel. What do they notice? Each of these sets forms an equilateral, or perfect, triangle on the color wheel. (You can take a few moments here to discuss different kinds of triangles.) Another way of looking at this is that triadic colors are *equally far apart on the wheel*. You might tell the class that we start color wheels by placing primary colors equally far apart.

Take a box of 24 Crayola crayons and empty them onto a table where everyone can see what you do. Explain that each box contains an 18-color color wheel and six non-color-wheel crayons. (I believe Crayola is the only brand that has a true 18-color color wheel in the box.) Ask them to pick the crayons that don't belong on a normal color wheel. Black, white, and gray are not colors, and brown is not found on the wheel. Pink is a value of red, and apricot (or peach, depending on the age of the box) is a tint of yellow-orange (or orange). Set those six crayons aside.

Take the red, yellow, and blue crayons and arrange them like the spokes of a wheel, equally far apart. Ask what color we get if we mix red and yellow. They should all reply "orange." Find the true orange crayon and place it halfway between the red and the yellow. Repeat the process for green and purple, placing them between the yellow and blue and red and blue crayons respectively. Ask what color we would expect to get if we mixed red and orange. Elicit both "red-orange" and "orange-red."

Now here comes the fun part. Up until a few years ago, a teacher could order a box of Crayola crayons in which the colors were labeled with their real names. Even though the boxes sold at your local store might sport cute names like dandelion instead of orange-yellow, a box purchased from a school supplier was educational as well as useful. Now, to my knowledge, there is no company that produces a box with a complete set of true, color wheel names. I (along with other art teachers) have complained to representatives from Binney & Smith and called the toll-free number on the crayon boxes to no avail. Perhaps if everyone who reads this book called . . . (It's 1-800-CRAYOLA or www. crayola.com, just in case you have a minute or two.)

Fortunately, the colors are still the same—only the names have been changed. So orange-red is now scarlet, orange-yellow is dandelion, (a scientific change from its former incarnation as "macaroni and cheese," a name that anyone can see is arbitrary), green-blue is cerulean, and violet-blue is indigo. I won't even begin to discuss how erroneous some of these terms are, although I do discuss it with my students. At any rate, you should be able to construct an 18-color color wheel out of the box by placing the crayons in the following way. Starting with the red crayon, the order is: red, orange-red (scarlet), red-orange, orange, yellow-orange, orange-yellow (dandelion), yellow, green-yellow, yellow-green, green, blue-green, green-blue (cerulean), blue, violet-blue (indigo), blue-violet, violet, red-violet, violet-red, and back to red. I go around the entire wheel asking for each pair of intermediates. "What goes between yellow and green? What goes between blue and green?" and so forth.

Once you have your "wheel" on the table, ask again for the definition of a triadic color scheme, and elicit the information that it consists of three colors equally far apart on the wheel. "What is 18 divided by three? That's right—six!" Pull the yellow crayon lightly out of the wheel. Use it as number one, and count off six crayons. This will bring you to red or blue. Pull it slightly out of the wheel, and using it as one, count to six again. This will bring you to the third primary. Repeat the procedure to prove that primaries are equally far apart. Slide the primaries back into the circle and pull out a secondary. Go around the wheel to prove that the secondaries form a triadic color scheme. Explain that we cannot just say that intermediates form a triadic scheme, because there are several possibilities. Pick an intermediate, slide it out, and repeat the procedure. Your results will be somewhat "primary-ish" or "secondary-ish." That is, if you start with green-blue (cerulean), your other two colors will be close to red and yellow: namely violet-red and orange-yellow (dandelion). If you start with red-orange, your other two colors will be close to violet and green, namely blue-violet and yellow-green. There are four different intermediate triadic color schemes on an 18-color wheel.

Make sure that each student is clear about the colors that he or she may use. If their crayon lines are a primary color, they may only use primaries in this section. If their crayon lines are a secondary color, they may only use secondaries. Although they may mix colors with values and use pure values, they may not mix colors with each other. That would create other colors that are not part of the color scheme. Students should pick one of the two remaining sections and color it with the usual materials. Remind them about using pure black and white in a balanced way.

Artists might choose a triadic color scheme when they want a lot of contrast without the vibrating effect of opposites.

Lesson 10: Analogous Color Schemes

Lesson Summary: Students will fill in the final section from Lesson 6 using an analogous color scheme.

Purpose: Students will learn the definition and effect of analogous colors.

Materials: Last 6″ × 9″ section from Lesson 6, crayons, markers, colored pencils, 12″ × 18″ white construction paper

Review: Color scheme, monochromatic, complementary, triadic, value, intensity, tint, shade

New Vocabulary/Concepts: Analogous, analogy, related, similar, simile, metaphor

Time: Three periods

Possible Visual Aids: Orazio Gentileschi, *The Lute Player*; several Vincent Van Goghs, such as *Wheat Field with Cyprus Trees, Starry Night,* and *Still Life Vase with 15 Sunflowers*

This is the last of the four basic schemes. (We don't cover split-complementary.) Students will use the same materials as in the previous three lessons.

After reviewing the three color schemes you have already presented, write the word "analogous" on the board and ask if anyone has heard this word or the word "analogy." Depending upon the age of your students, they might have encountered the term in language arts. Even my first graders have encountered analogies on standardized tests, although they may not know the term for them, and by grade two, the teacher uses the word and talks about such analogies as similes and metaphors. "Hat : head (hat is to head) as shoe : foot" is an example of analogous thinking on achievement tests. When things are analogous, they are similar or related in some way. (I cite the old commercial that proclaimed, "A breakfast without orange juice is like a day without sunshine.") After you have discussed and demonstrated this concept, go to the color wheel.

You might use the following script with younger children. "Colors can be related in different ways. If yellow married red, they would have orange children. You've all heard of genes. We each have some traits inherited from our fathers and some from our mothers, so if we mix red and yellow traits we get some kind of orangey result. This might be orange-yellow, yellow-orange, orange, red-orange, or orange-red. Red and yellow do not share any traits, but they can be related by marriage. There is another way colors can be related. Green, blue-green, green-blue, violet-blue, blue-violet, and violet are all 'children' of blue—they have blue traits in them. These two examples include groups of colors that lie in a row, next to each other, on the color wheel. But if we think about it, *all* colors lie in a row on the wheel. To have an analogous color scheme, we can begin from any color on the wheel and circle in one direction or the other, but we must stop when we reach a color that appears to be opposite of the color we started with. So I might start with red and go through violet-red, red-violet, violet, blue-violet, violet-blue, and blue, but I must stop there, because the next color has green in it, and green is the opposite of red. The number of colors in an analogous color scheme depends on the wheel I use. If my wheel includes only the primaries and secondaries, there will be three colors in my scheme. A 12-color wheel will have groups of five analogous colors, and an 18-color wheel will allow us seven hues. Since our boxes of crayons contain 18-color wheels, each of us may use up to 7 colors in this section, and each of you have three choices on the wheel. If your lines are a primary color, you may go from that primary clockwise through the intermediates and secondary to (and including) the next primary. You might go counterclockwise through the intermediates and secondary to (and including) the next primary. Or you might go through the intermediates to (and including) the secondaries on either side of your primary. So if your lines are red, for example, you could go from red to blue *or* from red to yellow *or* from purple to orange. If your lines are a secondary color, you could go from that secondary clockwise through the intermediates and primary to the next secondary *or* counterclockwise through the intermediates and primary to the next secondary *or* from the primary on one side of your secondary through the intermediates and your secondary to the primary on the other side."

When you are sure that everyone understands the nature of analogous colors, have them fill in the final section of the project using the usual materials. Students may mix colors. Any tertiaries created will be related to the colors used. Once again, students may alter the intensity or value of a color and use values as themselves.

Artists can use analogous color schemes to unify their works. This is not quite as restricting as a monochromatic plan.

When the student has completed all four quarters, glue them back together onto a piece of white 12″ by 18″ construction paper and put their name on the back.

Lesson 11: File and Free

See First Year, Lesson 13.

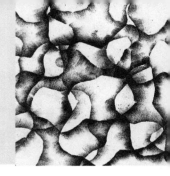

Unit Two: **Value**

Because of the nature of Lessons 6 through 11, you have already reviewed a great deal of material about value. The projects in this unit will therefore focus on aspects of this element that you have not stressed previously.

Lesson 12: **Reviewing Value**

Lesson Summary: After a review of the element, students will create a pencil drawing that displays a variety of values.

Purpose: This lesson will reinforce the students' knowledge of the element "value" and add to their understanding of its uses, especially in creating a feeling of depth.

Materials: 12″ × 18″ white construction or drawing paper, pencils

Review: Element, value, tint, shade, three properties of color, black, white, gray, gradation, form

Time: One+ period

Possible Visual Aids: Peter Paul Rubens, *Head of a Boy;* Albrecht Durer, *Young Hare*, *Bernardo Luini, Head of a Woman*

Begin with a brief review of the terms you have stressed in the color scheme projects: value, tint, and shade. Then continue with something like the following.

"There are essentially three ways we refer to value. First, each color has its own value. That is, if we look at a color wheel or open a box of crayons or markers, we will immediately notice that some colors are lighter than others. In its pure state, what we might call straight-out-of-the-rainbow, yellow simply reflects more light back to our eyes than violet, orange is lighter than blue, and so forth. Some colors are very similar in value.

"Second, we can change the value of any given color. We can make blue lighter or darker by adding white or black. So we can discuss value by referring to tints or shades, and we covered that pretty thoroughly in the color scheme lessons.

"Finally, we can discuss value in its pure state, which is why it is a separate element and not just a property of color. We certainly talked about black, white, and gray in the earlier lessons, but in this unit, we are going to focus on a use of value that is vital to artists who wish to create an illusion of depth or form." You might want to review the definition of "illusion" before proceeding.

Hold up an example of a realistically shaded sphere. (See sphere from First Year.) Explain that an artist cannot draw a sphere without using gradation or shading. Review the concept of gradation. (See First Year, Lesson 15.) The artist can get us to see a cube or cylinder or cone by using line only, but a sphere without shading is merely a flat circular shape.

Using a pencil, demonstrate gradation. You might also want to put up some examples of artworks that display this principle. Realistic still lifes would work well. Point out the three-dimensional effect created by the use of light and dark.

Pass out 12″ by 18″ white paper. Ask the students to spend the rest of the period creating a drawing or design with pencil that uses a wide variety of values and includes at least one example of gradation. While lines alone may get lighter and darker, encourage them to fill in areas with value.

The time you allow for this project will depend on your schedule and the age of your students. Since the drawing requires only a pencil, it is a simple piece to work on while classmates are finishing the future lessons. This is another great opportunity for observational drawing.

Lesson 13: Charcoal Value 3-D Effects

Lesson Summary: Students will create a three-dimensional effect using only value.

Purpose: Students will see how darker values tend to recede and lighter values tend to come forward.

Materials: 12″ × 18″ white construction paper, 12″ × 18″ manila paper, charcoal sticks, scissors, pencils (for names only)

Review: Value (definition), illusion, kinds of shapes, overlap, contrast, gradation

New Vocabulary/Concept: Using value to create the illusion of depth

Time: Approximately three periods

Possible Visual Aids: Works by Juan Gris, such as *Guitar* and *Portrait of Picasso*

Softer, chunkier charcoal is better for this project than vine charcoal. I usually buy a box of 12 square, 3″ sticks and break each stick in half. A shorter piece is actually easier to use.

Begin with the usual review, stressing the fact that values can make things seem nearer or farther away. Our eye tends to see lighter values and colors as closer than darker ones. Of course, this is not always true, but shadows and parts of objects that go away from us are usually rendered in lower values than fronts of things. You might show some visual aids to reinforce this concept, like Honore Daumier's *The Print Collector*. Remind the students of the shading on the sphere and how it made the object look three-dimensional. Value is frequently used to make objects have the illusion of depth. This project is going to create just such a magical illusion.

Have the students gather around a desk or table in such a way that everyone can see your demonstration. On the table, you will have a piece of manila paper, a piece of 12″ by 18″ white construction paper, scissors, and a piece of charcoal. Your first step will be to cut a shape from the side or corner of the manila paper. This shape will serve as a template. Explain that they will be using the remainder of the manila for something else, so they should not cut the shape out of the middle. They may make any kind of shape—geometric, organic, or irregular—but it should not be fragile. Ask for a definition of that word, and elicit the fact that it means "easily broken." In our case, it means "easily torn." Draw some examples on the board that have tenuous arms or narrow necks, such as those shown below. Explain that they are going to be pretty hard on these shapes, and they want to create something sturdy. The shape should be about the size of the palm of a hand or a little larger.

Fragile shapes.

Place your template in the center of the remaining manila. With the charcoal, create a band of black around the edge of the shape about a quarter of an inch wide. Carefully place the shape on the white paper. Holding the template in place with one or two fingertips in the center, gently but firmly push the charcoal off the shape on to the white paper with one or two fingertips of the other hand. Go completely around the shape, and do not skip any spots. Do not rub back and forth. Lift your fingers and stroke from the inside of the shape out onto the white. When you have gone all the way around, carefully lift the shape off the white paper and place it back on the manila. The charcoaled area will appear to be a shadow cast by a white shape that seems to be higher than the remaining white background.

Rechalk the shape and place it on the white paper again in such a way that it overlaps a good portion of the first tracing. Repeat the rubbing procedure, once again being sure to go completely around the shape. Lift the template carefully and place it back on the manila. The shape created by the overlap will appear to be whiter than the rest and will seem to pop out from the page. Explain that they will repeat this process until the entire page is covered. There should be no meandering negative spaces, and overlaps should always be substantial. The template may go off the page. Students should press firmly but not too hard, as that would leave oily fingerprints around the shape. They should not spread the charcoal out too far with each stroke, because there will be no pure white areas left on the paper. The cleaner (and therefore lighter) the white is, the more it will pop off the page, or appear to come forward. Stress how important it is to rechalk the template after

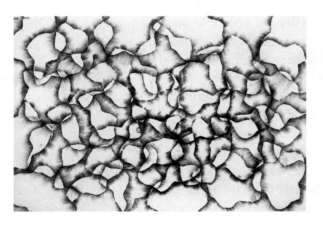

···

These works by second graders Sarah George, Timothy Geisse, and Olivia Adams display the lovely results you can achieve with this lesson.

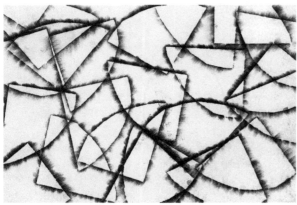

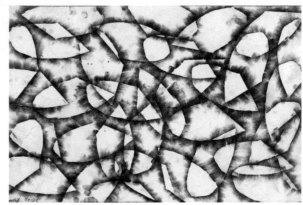

each use. Although as the project progresses, the edges will appear to be very black and have lots of charcoal on them, they will not produce a richly dark halo unless they are constantly refreshed. You can tell when a student stops rechalking, because the "shadows" become lighter and it throws off the balance of the piece.

Children may turn the paper either way. It is vital that they place their names on the front before they begin, while their hands are clean. Names should be small, and students may brush charcoal over them if the composition requires it. It is a good idea to hand out the charcoal only after you have OKed the cut shape and the student is ready to begin chalking.

Lesson 14: Value as Tint and Shade

Lesson Summary: Students will use a painted montage to create a piece with strong value structure.

Purpose: Students will learn how important values are in the creation of composition.

Materials: 12″ × 18″ construction paper in white, black, and two grays, newspaper (optional), various two-dimensional materials that display pure values (optional), scissors, glue, watercolors and brushes, water buckets, paper towels, pencils

Review: Value, intensity, tint, shade, tone, collage/montage, wash

New Vocabulary/Concept: Value as a factor of compositional balance

Time: Approximately four periods

Possible Visual Aids: Horace Pippin, *The Domino Players*, Paul Cornoyer, *Plaza After Rain;* Henry Tanner, *Banjo Lesson;* Theodore Gericault, *Raft of the Medusa*

Due to time constraints, I have not done this project for several years, but it is an enjoyable and instructive way to work with tints and shades. If your schedule permits, I would recommend it. You will begin with the usual review and do a demonstration.

You will need black, light gray, dark gray, and white 12″ by 18″ construction paper, and you might also use the print portion (no color) of newspapers. Point out that areas of print can be seen as gray. You might use other materials that have pure value, such as tape, doilies, or wrapping paper. While we always used the white paper as the background, you could actually use any of the construction paper values in that capacity.

There are two distinctive steps to this lesson. In step one, the students glue shapes cut from the various values of construction paper (and other materials, if included) on the chosen background to create a picture or design. This should be extremely well composed and balanced, especially as to darks and lights. Make sure that the edges of all the pieces are carefully glued—nothing should be loose.

Step two requires watercolors. The students may use anything in the paint box except the black, and they should not use the pigments too thickly. The value structure will be provided by the underlying montage. The pupils will simply paint a picture or design right on top of the picture or design they created with the cut and glued papers. They should be encouraged to go off the underlying shapes. That is, an area of color should cross several values. The students should also use relatively thin washes that allow the values to show through. For example, in your demonstration, you might put clouds of grays, newspaper, and black on a white area, then paint the entire sky with a thin wash of orange or blue. The easiest approach to this project is to paint an abstract design over a different, albeit related, design. Where the wash goes over white paper, you will create a tint. Where it covers black or dark gray paper, it will yield a shade. Gray papers can also yield a less intense tone. You might need to touch up the gluing after the paint has dried.

Lesson 15: File and Free

See First Year, Lesson 13.

Unit Three: **Texture**

Texture is not a particularly complicated element, and we explored it in some depth during year one, so this unit will not be lengthy.

Lesson 16: **Review of Texture and Watercolor Resist Crumble**

> **Lesson Summary:** Students will create a textured project using a crayon resist technique.
>
> **Purpose:** Students will explore the third way that artists use texture in an artwork: texture of the medium.
>
> **Materials:** 9″ × 12″ white construction paper, crayons, watercolors, brushes, 12″ × 18″ manila paper, water buckets, paper towels
>
> **Review:** Element, texture, definition, real, illusion, collage, sculpture, medium
>
> **New Vocabulary/Concepts:** Texture of the medium, batik (optional)
>
> **Time:** Four to five periods
>
> **Possible Visual Aids:** Works by Claude Monet, Georges Seurat, or Vincent Van Gogh; possibly a real piece of batik

The first period of this lesson will be used for review and demonstration. The project itself requires crayons and watercolor. For the review, it will be very helpful to have three visual aids. One should be an example of a realistic painting with a wide variety of implied textures, such as *Portrait of Prince Jacques Grimaldi*, by Nicholas de Largilliere; one should be an image of (or a real) sculpture or collage, such as Mayan bas reliefs; and for the third, you might use a print of Claude Monet's *Le Jardin de Monet á Giverny* or a similar image.

As always, when starting a new unit, review the names and nature of elements of art. After revealing that the element to be covered will be texture, ask if anyone remembers its definition. Hopefully, someone will recall that it means "the way something feels or the way it looks like it would feel." Write the definition on the board and discuss the various types of artists who deal with real textures: sculptors, architects, fabric designers, furniture designers, collage artists, and so forth. Some things feel exactly the way they appear to feel. I need not pet a cat to know that it is, in fact, as furry as it looks. Refer to the sculptural visual aid.

Show the realistic painting and ask, "If you were allowed to touch this painting in a museum (which of course you wouldn't!), would it feel like velvet and fur and lace (or whatever textures appear in your example)? No! It would feel smooth. What do we call it when the artist tricks our eye this way? That's right—illusion!" Write the word on the board and discuss illusion a little. (See First Year, Lesson 21.) Ask which artists use illusion in their work: painters, wallpaper designers, some flooring designers, plastic laminate designers, and so forth.

Explain that there is a third way that artists use texture. Focus on the print of the Monet. "If the artist who painted the realistic painting had done this one, it would look very different. We would know exactly what fabrics the lady was wearing and we would feel the texture of each flower petal. The grass would look grassy and the leaves would look leafy. But what texture do we notice in this painting? That's right, the paint itself. The flowers, grass, clothing, and leaves all have the same texture. In the realistic work, the artist has been very careful to hide the brushstrokes, but in the Monet, the artist wants us to be aware of his process, and the texture we notice is *the texture of the materials*, in this case, the paint. Does anyone remember the word we use for materials?" Elicit the word "medium," and write it on the board.

After discussing this until everyone grasps the concept, demonstrate the project. On a piece of 9″ by 12″ white construction paper, color several shapes heavily with crayon. Make these fairly good-sized. Make sure one of them is white. Explain that this is a crayon resist project, the same technique they used for their second color mixing lesson, so it is important that they make the crayon waxy. But this is sort of a reverse of that project. Instead of coloring the lines and leaving the spaces empty, they are to color the shapes in and leave a little space or line between them. They may also leave background negative space if it's not too much of the page.

In this project, they have three choices for the watercolor: black, purple, or blue. They must think about this before they start using their crayons, because if they choose black they must not use black crayon, if they use blue they should stay away from bluish crayons, and if they choose to use purple they should avoid purplish crayons, especially violet and blue-violet. Red-violet is fine. If they use a crayon that is too close in color to their paint, that shape will essentially disappear when the paint goes on. At the very best, the balance of the project will change. Some of my students like to literally remove their forbidden crayons from their box while they work so they don't forget. Remind the children that if they use white, it is hard to make sure it is waxy and solid, and they must balance such shapes carefully.

I usually use purple paint in my demo, so I purposely put a violet and blue-violet crayon shape on my page so the children can see the problem at the end. I explain that lighter, brighter colors will work the best, so I make several shapes using the warmer, lighter colors in the box.

I tell them that they may draw a picture or a design. They might, for instance, color a bunch of fish, leaving the background uncolored, then use blue or purple paint to represent the water. Or they could fill the entire page with shapes, leaving only the small spaces between the colors.

Now comes the fun part. Remind the students how you are always telling them to be very careful with their projects—not to wrinkle or smear or make marks on them. Go to the sink, and run your demonstration page under the cold water quickly, front and back. Then wad it up into a fairly tight ball. (I usually make a big production of "ruining" the piece.) Open the wad very carefully. There may well be some tears in the paper. These will heal as the project dries. Place the opened piece on a piece of 12″ by 18″ manila paper and cover the shapes with a layer of watercolor. The paint should not be too thick, so that it does not resist, but it should be very rich. It will dry lighter, and you want the black to dry black and the purple or blue to be fairly true. If your paint lightens too much, the project will be very dull. Make sure to go over the crayon shapes, not around them. On student projects, the paint should cover the entire page.

The result of this technique should be a batik-type webbing effect. You might discuss the process of batik, or even show an actual example. Point out that this texture covers the whole picture. Even if they drew a cat lying on a braided rug that sits on a wooden floor in front of a brick fireplace, the texture of the picture will all be the same. The crumbling will crack the crayon and the paper as well, and the paint should be darker in the cracks. The texture is the texture of the materials, or technique, not of the individual items or shapes in the image.

Second graders Maddie Clements and Mike Johnson created these great paper "batiks."

A few tips about this particular project. Be sure to try it before class. Over the years, the quality of the paper and paint has changed, so practice with your materials. Students should put their names on the back in waxy, light-colored crayon, because the paint will bleed through and obscure pencil.

Finally, I would not wet and crumble a student's project too close to the end of the period. You want each piece to be completely painted in one period, so you don't have to rewet it the next time. Depending on the age of your students, they will probably require 10 to 15 minutes for this step. I simply stack finished crayon projects, let those students free draw, and set out that group of projects at the beginning of the following period. If you must stop in the middle of painting, just rewet it the next time, do not crumble it again. The wet projects will be very fragile, so leave them on the manila when placing them on the drying rack.

Lesson 17: Relation of Texture to Pattern

Lesson Summary: Students will create the shapes of a composition by drawing patterns and textures.

Purpose: The project will introduce the ideas of motif and contrast and reinforce the concepts of pattern and texture.

Materials: 9″ × 12″ white construction paper, pencil, black marker (regular or thin)

Review: Texture, pattern, principle, regular, random, repetition

New Vocabulary/Concepts: Motif, contrast

Time: One to three periods

Possible Visual Aids: Quilts, story quilts by Faith Ringgold, adire cloth of Yoruba people

This project not only helps reinforce a concept discussed in first grade, it also shows the importance of the principle of contrast in a work of art. Before presenting it, carefully reread Lesson 24 of the first-year curriculum. You may use a regular black marker or a thin one.

Review the nature of texture, and ask if anyone remembers what principle of art is closely related to it. Remind everyone what a principle is and how it differs from an element.

Discuss the way in which pattern and texture are similar. They both require repetition, which is also a principle of art. Review regular and random patterns.

Explain that if we looked at a texture under a magnifying glass or microscope, it would appear to be a pattern. Likewise, if we viewed a pattern from a distance, it might appear to be a texture. There is no precise way to say when something stops being a pattern and becomes a texture or vice versa. The best way to decide if something qualifies as a texture is to ask yourself if it makes you want to touch it. If you think of an area as furry or bumpy or rough, then it is a texture. If you are more aware of the repetition, it is a pattern.

A pattern is created through the repetition of a motif. The motif can be virtually any element of art or a combination of them. If you repeat your name over and over, your name is the motif. (The letters can be considered lines or shapes.) In a polka-dot fabric, a single dot is the motif. On the American flag, the motif for the stripes would be one red and one white. Discuss the fact that motifs occur in music and literature. In music, the word refers to a series of notes that are repeated, and in literature, it is a theme.

Put a piece of 9″ by 12″ white construction paper on the board. Explain that the first step of this project involves using *very light* pencil lines to tessellate the page. Demonstrate in such a way that students can barely see your lines. (Or better yet, not see them at all.) The shapes you create should not be too big or too small. Patterns and textures require repetition, and you can't repeat a motif enough if the area is too small.

Tell the students that they are going to fill each shape with a pattern or a texture. The scale and the motif will determine whether we see it as a pattern or a texture. Using a black marker, fill one of the shapes with a repeated motif, like a dot. Go carefully up to the pencil lines but not beyond, and use plenty of repetition to fill the area fully. Think of the shape as a piece cut from cloth. Ask the class if they can see the shape now. Fill an adjacent shape with a different motif, like a line. Stress the fact that shapes next to each other must have patterns or textures that are very different or the shape will not show. Letters, numbers, and even punctuation marks can be motifs, but if you use such motifs next to each other, it will be very hard to see where one shape ends and the next begins.

Ask if anyone knows what the word "contrast" means, and elicit that it is another word for "difference." The most important kind of contrast for this project is a contrast of value. That is, when two patterns or textures lie next to each other, one should be much darker than the other. This can be achieved by using heavier lines or dots, or a denser use of the motif. The important thing is to fill the shape, not just put a few motifs in the center. Also, you should remind the students not to draw on the pencil lines. The only way we should know where one shape ends and another begins is by the change of pattern or texture.

The other problem you should mention is the use of something that is not truly repetition of a motif. A zigzag line might fill the shape (see Figure 1), but it is not really a pattern, and it is certainly not a texture. Show how it can be changed into a pattern/texture (see Figure 2). One of something is not a pattern. One bump is not a texture. One stripe does not make a pattern.

Once you have explained the project, pass out the paper and begin. Because this project usually comes near spring break, I frequently let students start it in class and then send it home to do over vacation. Since it requires only a black marker at that point, it is a terrific project to take on a plane or in a car, and it can even be done while sitting in front of a television.

Figure 1   Figure 2

Lesson 18: File and Free

See First Year, Lesson 13.

Unit Four: **Shape**

While we focus on elements in the first two years, we also deal with many principles. Symmetry, overlapping, contrast, similarity, repetition, pattern, and negative versus positive space are all principles. This unit will not only help reinforce the definitions associated with shape that were covered in the first year, it will also introduce another principle.

Lesson 19: **Review of Shape— Focus on Positive and Negative**

Lesson Summary: Students will create a symmetrical design using cut paper and glue.

Purpose: This project will reinforce vocabulary learned the previous year and focus on the nature of positive and negative shape.

Materials: 9″ × 12″ and 12″ × 18″ construction paper in several colors, scissors, glue stick, pencils, X-Acto-type blade (for teacher)

Review: Element, shape, geometric, organic, irregular, positive space, negative space, symmetry

Time: Three to four periods

Possible Visual Aids: Chinese Tao' T'ieh figure, symmetrical tribal masks or carvings

You will need several colors and values of construction paper for this project, some 9″ by 12″ and some 12″ by 18″.

After reviewing the elements of art and revealing that shape will be the topic for this unit, go over the definition of shape and ask what different kinds of shapes artists use. Elicit the definitions of geometric, organic, and irregular before reviewing the nature of positive and negative space. Then proceed to the demonstration.

On a 9″ by 12″ piece of construction paper placed *in the portrait position*, draw a picture or design lightly in pencil, using only shapes. No shape may touch any other shape or an outside edge, although you may create shapes that are entirely inside other shapes. You may use any kind of shape, geometric, irregular, or organic, but the figures may not be too small or too convoluted. Explain to the students that they are going to cut out the shapes without coming in from the edge or going from piece to piece, and very small or extremely wiggly shapes will not allow their scissors to turn.

Start the shapes by making a small slit with a sharp blade along each outline. This avoids big puncture holes and a lot of tearing. Then cut the shapes out carefully, being sure not to trim anything off or cut through the negative space in any way. When you are finished, you should have one continuous negative shape and all of the cutout pieces, which, when placed back together like a puzzle, should reveal no gaps. Stress that they are not to trim anything. If they go off a pencil line, they will simply adjust the edge of the shape accordingly. You might demonstrate this by making an exaggerated "oops" and coming back to your original line as soon as possible.

Hold up the large background and ask what it is. Elicit the term "negative shape" before you continue.

Place a piece of 12″ by 18″ paper in a highly contrasting value in landscape position. Place the negative shape carefully on one half of this, so that the 12″ sides are aligned. If any of your shapes have interior shapes, fit only those shapes with holes back into place. Using a glue stick, fill the hole with paste and fit the interior shape carefully into place. When all the interior shapes are

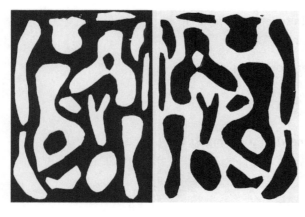

glued down, flip the 9″ by 12″ background space carefully over like a book page and line it up along the opposite edge of the 12″ by 18″ paper. Then place all of the pieces, both with holes and without, perfectly into position. If a puzzle piece is solid, simply lift it up, place the glue in the space underneath, and press it down. If the piece has a hole in it, the glue must be applied to its back. Remind the students that they must glue the correct side.

Once all the remaining pieces are in place, put glue on top of the loose background area and then flip it once again like a book page over onto the other side. Putting the glue on first will help avoid gluing the wrong side. If a student has only solid pieces, you simply skip the first gluing step.

Hold up your demonstration, and ask what we call this kind of arrangement. The students should recognize the symmetry of the piece. Review symmetry briefly. Then point to the side on which you glued the big background shape, and ask, "On this side, which is the negative shape?" This is an interesting question, because even though you actually placed the "leftover" piece on the paper like a positive shape, we tend to read such uninterrupted areas as negative space.

This review and demonstration usually takes one period, so you can begin the actual project when the students return. Simply allow them to choose a piece of paper and begin. Because they will be using both sides of the page, they should make their names very small in a corner. You will need to start their shapes for them with a blade. Of course, older students might start their own shapes, depending on the rules of your classroom. At cleanup time, make a sandwich with the 12″ by 18″ paper as the bottom, the small shapes as the filling, and the background shape as the top.

Lesson 20: Distortion

Lesson Summary: Students will be introduced to distortion, and they will alternate strips of two different images to create a piece that appears different from different points of view.

Purpose: Students will learn about and create distortion.

Materials: 9″ × 12″ and 12″ × 18″ construction papers in light colors and values, markers, pencils (for names only, unless lining off backs manually), scissors, glue sticks, white crayons (optional)

Review: Shape, geometric, irregular, organic, positive and negative space, landscape and portrait orientation

New Vocabulary/Concept: Distortion

Time: Approximately four to five periods

Possible Visual Aids: Sculptures by Alberto Giacometti, medieval art

I have several things in my classroom that can demonstrate distortion. Many of these items were made by my eighth graders several years ago in response to an assignment, but you could replicate them easily. One involves drawing simple pictures, like the outline of a shark or a dolphin—or any shape, actually—on pieces of very stretchy white fabric using an appropriate pen. Another results from breaking up a mirror tile and gluing the pieces onto a background, leaving a slight space between the pieces. I also recommend having at least one of those glass blocks used in building. You will need a wide variety of 9″ by 12″ and 12″ by 18″ pieces of pale colored and white construction paper.

After reviewing the element under discussion, the various kinds of shapes an artist might use, and the idea of positive and negative space, write the word "distortion" on the board and ask if anyone knows its meaning. You might introduce the idea by referring to the mirrors one sees at carnivals. We fortunately have these mirrors at our local children's museum, so most of my students are familiar with them, but if your pupils are not, you can open your discussion using one or more of the objects mentioned.

The key aspect of distortion is that you should understand that it *is* a distortion—you must know what the original object is. For instance, if you draw an amoeba-like shape on the board, no one knows if it is meant to be a distorted circle or simply an organic shape. If you draw a squiggly human-esque shape, however, the children will know it is a distorted human figure before you are halfway around it. In art, as well as in the dictionary, distortion usually refers to shape or form, although we can distort virtually any element. Distortion is a little hard to put into words, but essentially it means to change something from its natural appearance in such a way that we can still tell what it originally was. This is a good time to introduce (or repeat) the visual aids you have brought in. Hold the fabric in such a way that the shark or dolphin (or whatever) looks normal, and then stretch. The image still looks like a shark or dolphin, but it is longer or fatter. When the children look in the broken mirror, they can see their reflections, but their faces are cracked. If they look through a glass block, the view will be considerably distorted.

Explain that the word does not just apply to art. We can distort the truth. If they go fishing and catch a 10-inch bass, but tell their friends it was "this big" (hold your hands about two feet apart), they are exaggerating. Exaggeration is a form of distortion. I tell a funny, very dramatic story about a newspaper report on a slow news day. You can craft your own example.

We can also distort sound. Many students are familiar with the electronic gizmos that change the sound of guitars or voices. I discuss the fact that in the old days, records had three speeds. For fun, children would play records at the wrong speed, making them sound slow and deep or something like the "Chipmunks." Of course, I act this out!

Once the class is comfortable with the concept of distortion, you will begin to explain the project. For this particular lesson, you need not make the piece in class. Simply discuss the steps, but be sure to have a finished example to show them at the end.

Show the class a wide variety of very light and white 9″ by 12″ construction papers. If cost is an issue and you can't afford a large choice, you might choose only two or three, perhaps white and light gray. I use white, pale gray, light purple, pink, pale blue, peach, and pale green, as well as a few other random light colors from the storeroom.

Explain that they will each start with one piece of paper. They are to place the page in the portrait position and fill it with a picture or design using markers. This image should be predominantly filled-in shapes, and it should stretch completely across the paper. It need not actually touch the sides, but it should come close. There should be no little, teeny-tiny shapes. They may leave negative space (or not), but most of the paper should be covered with marker.

Once this first page is done, they are to pick a second sheet of 9″ by 12″ paper. This second sheet may be any color or value except the one they used for the first picture. They are to repeat the instructions for the first image: paper in portrait position, picture or design that fills most of the page, stretching from side to side, no teeny shapes, and so forth. If they did a design for the first piece, the second piece may be a similar design, a very different design, or a picture of something. If the first piece was a picture, the second might be a similar or related picture. For instance, one image might be a dog and the other a doghouse. One might be a house in summer, and the other might be the same house in winter. Or the second image might be a completely unrelated picture or a design.

While this project will result in distorted shapes, you might also point out that we will see distorted colors as well. If they mix yellow and blue paint, they simply see green, not a distorted yellow or blue. But if they try to draw a yellow sun with markers on light blue paper, the viewer will recognize that the sun was intended to be yellow and will read the color as distorted. The only surface that will reflect only true colors to our eyes is white.

After a student has finished a page, you are going to line off the back in one-inch vertical strips. The easiest way to do this is to line off a piece of white, 9″ by 12″ paper and place it on a copy machine. Simply turn the projects upside down and feed them in from the fold-down ledge that accommodates single pages. Make sure the papers are aligned properly. If you do not have access to a copier, or yours cannot handle construction paper, there is another way to save time. Cut a piece of sturdy cardboard that measures 12″ by a fraction less than one inch. While the children are working, you can line off their projects. After the back of the page is divided, number the strips from one to nine, *starting on the right-hand side*. Looking at the back of the drawing, the first number on the left is 9 and the last one on the right is 1.

If students want white in their images, and they are not using white paper, they should outline the desired shape in marker and color it with white crayon. If you are using a copier to make the lines, have them put the crayon on after the lines are done, as the copier will melt the crayon.

Meanwhile, back to the demonstration. On the board, draw two rectangles in the portrait position, and line them off quickly into nine sections. Number the sections in the same way as described to show the students what the backs of their papers will look like. Hold up a piece of 12″ by 18″ paper and tell them that, when they are done with their two images, each one of them will get a piece like this that matches one of their two pages. Draw another, larger rectangle on the board in the landscape position to represent this 12″ by 18″ piece.

Explain that they may start with either drawing. Let's say they chose pink and blue paper, and they choose to start with the pink page. They should carefully cut off strip number one from the pink paper. This will be on the right-hand side of the back, but when they turn the strip over, it will be the first strip on the left of the front. They are to line this strip up carefully along the left edge of the 12″ by 18″ paper and glue it down. Draw a strip on the left-hand side of your diagram and label it "1p." Then they are to cut piece number one from the blue paper and glue it carefully next to the pink piece. Draw a second strip and label it "1b." Tell them that it is very important not to leave gaps between the pieces and not to overlap. The more carefully and straight they cut, the easier this will be. They should continue cutting and gluing *one piece at a time*, alternating pictures, until the entire 12″ by 18″ piece is covered. Warn them that the last strip will probably not fit completely on the background. They should put the glue on the part of the background paper that is exposed and let the strip hang over. They should not trim anything off. They should also line the tops of the strips with the top of the background so that they line up correctly.

Explain that, after all their strips are glued down, you are going to fanfold the project. Then hold up the example you have prepared and demonstrate that, when they look at the piece from one direction, they will see one of their original images, and when they look at it from the other direction, they will see the other image. As they move across the front of the project, the images will become more and more distorted until they merge.

Older students may adapt this project in a number of ways. They can line off and number their own pages, use the same color or value for both sheets, or simply use two magazine or computer pictures. The only requirements are that the two images must be the same size, the strips must be uniform, and the background must be equal to the width of the two images side by side.

Anne Havlik created this excellent distortion project. (See color insert)

Lesson 21:   Tessellations

Lesson Summary: The students will create a design exhibiting technical tessellation.

Purpose: Students will learn about the geometry of true tessellations.

Materials: 12″ × 18″ white construction paper, 3″ × 5″ index cards, tape, pencils, crayons, colored pencils, or markers

Review: Shape, geometric, organic, irregular, positive and negative space, tessellation

New Vocabulary/Concept: Technical tessellation

Time: Three periods

Possible Visual Aids: The works of M. C. Escher

I no longer include this project because my students do it in their math classes, but I offer it here for those of you who would like to use it.

Most math and art teachers are probably familiar with the works of M. C. Escher. An artist and a mathematician, he is famous for his creative tessellations and the wonderful optical illusions he devised through his complete mastery of the theories of perspective. Posters and slides of his work are easily obtainable from a variety of sources. Even small children can do simple tessellations, and there are several books that can guide you in creating such a lesson.

A tessellation, as we have discussed earlier, is a design in which there is no leftover space—all the positive shapes fit together like a puzzle. You might want to focus on the difference between generally tessellating a page and technical tessellations, like those of Escher. A checkerboard is one example, and the geometric patterns used in much Arabic art and architecture provide many others. Floor tiles and ceiling tiles are usually handy examples.

Math teachers may already be quite conversant with the steps involved in creating such patterns, but here is an extremely basic project used by Jan Kendall and Elaine Sandy with Sycamore first graders. After your review of shape terms and tessellation, simply demonstrate it to your students.

Using a small index card, cut a shape out of the top. Slide the cutout piece carefully to the bottom of the card directly below its original location and tape it into position. (The flat top of the cutout piece will fit perfectly against the flat bottom of the card, as in Figure 1.) Place the card in the upper corner

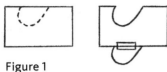

Figure 1

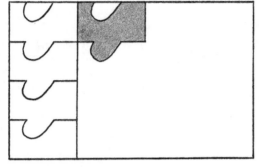

Figure 2

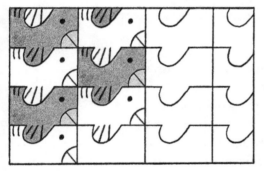

Figure 3

of a piece of 12″ by 18″ construction paper, lining up the top and one side of the card with the edges of the paper. Trace the parts of the shape not formed by the edges of the paper. (See Figure 2) Move the card down the side of the page until it lies directly below your first drawing. It should fit like a puzzle piece. Trace the parts that are not already formed by the previous tracing and the edge of the paper. Continue until you reach the bottom. If parts hang off, ignore them. Move the card back to the top of the page and place it exactly against the drawn side of the first shape. Trace any necessary parts and repeat the process until you have filled the entire page. (See Figure 3) Fill the shapes with crayon, marker, or colored pencil, using contrasting colors in a checkerboard arrangement. When the students do this project, ask them if their shapes look like anything—perhaps a bird or a train. They might choose to embellish their drawings *á la* Escher by adding a few details like windows or eyes.

Of course, this basic idea may be elaborated in a number of ways. You can cut pieces from a side or bottom or from more than one edge of the card. There are different types of tessellations and you might choose to focus on one of them. For further information, check out a book like *Mosaic and Tessellated Patterns: How to Create Them* by John Wilson, or any similar source. There are a wide variety of posters, videos, books, and CD-ROMs available on the subject.

Lesson 22: File and Free

See First Year, Lesson 13.

Unit Five: **Line**

As I explained in the introduction, some of these units will be very brief. There is not a great deal of esoteric vocabulary associated with line, so this section is quite short. Later in my curriculum, my students practice blind contour and gesture drawing. We discuss "lost and found" line and explore the effects of various types of line on famous artworks. However, in these earlier grades, we focus predominantly on contour and calligraphic lines.

Lesson 23: Review of Line—Using Line to Create the Illusion of Form

Lesson Summary: Students will create the illusion of form using simple contour lines.

Purpose: Students will learn a technique for creating the illusion of depth and explore contour lines more fully.

Materials: 9″ × 12″ white construction paper (or 8½″ × 11″ computer paper), pencils, markers in dark values (don't use yellow)

Review: Elements, line (definition), dimensions, contour, calligraphic, direction, illusion, form

New Vocabulary/Concept: Contour map

Time: Two periods

Possible Visual Aids: Contour map; M. C. Escher, *Rind*

Briefly review the elements of art and explain that you are going to talk about line. Ask if anyone remembers its definition, and elicit the response that it is "the path of a moving point." Discuss the various concepts covered in the first year Lessons 34 through 38: dimensions, direction, movement, contour lines, calligraphic lines, outlines, and so forth. Pay particular attention to the review of the term "contour." Remind students that it refers to the shape or form of something. Ask if any of them have seen a contour map. If you have access to one, you might use it as a visual aid. Review the definition of "contour lines"—lines that never get wider or narrower. Explain that they are going to use contour lines to create the illusion of form. You will probably want to review the definition of "illusion" and talk briefly about the fact that a form has thickness.

For your demonstration, place a piece of 9″ by 12″ white paper on the board in the portrait position. Place your nondominant hand and bare forearm on the page in such a way that it fills the paper nicely. Splay your fingers slightly, but make sure your thumb is generally vertical, not parallel to the top of the page. Trace your hand and arm very lightly with a pencil.

Using a dark value marker, start at the bottom of the page and draw a straight contour line parallel to the lower edge. When you come to a pencil line, *starting right on the pencil line*, curve the line up slightly. Come down *on* the next pencil line, and continue parallel to the lower edge until the end of the page. Try to align this part of the straight line with the starting line. Repeat the process about a quarter-inch above the first. Continue up the page, keeping all the straight, horizontal lines as parallel to each other as possible. When you come to fingers, the theory is the same. Curve up on the first pencil line, down onto the second, up on the third, down onto the forth, and so forth. All lines traversing negative space should be parallel to the top or bottom.

Even second graders can create fabulous results, as evidenced in this work by Cecile Blahunka.

Actually, you need not start at the top or bottom of the page. You could start in the middle and move up and down. If time is a factor, you can simply draw enough central lines to demonstrate the technique and show a finished piece you created beforehand. One nice aspect of this project is that a student can fill in large gaps without going completely across the page, and it will not be particularly noticeable. Be sure the marker lines change direction sharply on the pencil lines, not somewhere in the general vicinity.

Lesson 24: Calligraphic Lines

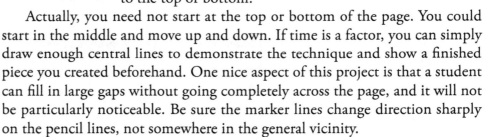

Lesson Summary: Children will practice making calligraphic lines.

Purpose: Students will learn the theory behind making calligraphic lines and observe their effect.

Materials: 12″ × 18″ paper (or newspaper or 3′-wide roll paper), black tempera paint, shallow containers, bulldog clamps (one per student), felt, pencils (for names only)

Review: Line (definition), contour, calligraphic

New Vocabulary/Concept: Calligraphy

Time: One period

Possible Visual Aids: Calligraphy examples, possibly medieval

This is an optional lesson, but it is a fun way to explore calligraphic line if your schedule and budget permit.

Review line vocabulary, reminding students that calligraphic lines get wider and narrower. Calligraphy is the art of beautiful writing, and it usually involves special pens and brushes. This approach may be a little easier for small hands, and it could also offer more freedom to older students.

You will need enough bulldog clamps for each child to have one and some thick felt. Bulldog clamps come in different sizes, and you might want to offer an assortment and let the children share. I have found that the smallest ones work the best. In fact, the best size usually has magnets attached. Since these can get in the way, you might want to use the clips that you buy in office supply stores for holding papers together. For each clamp, cut a piece of felt the same width as that clamp and approximately one-inch long. Clip it in such a way that about ¼" to ⅜" hangs out the "jaws."

Place several shallow containers of black tempera paint where students can reach them easily. Styrofoam meat trays or the plastic containers from frozen microwave meals work well. You might want to thin the paint slightly.

Do a very brief demonstration. It would probably be best to place your paper flat on a table rather than on the board. Dip the exposed felt in the paint and show the students that if they place the edge of the felt on the page parallel to the top and pull the clamp straight down the paper, they will get a broad line as wide as the "brush." If they place the clamp in the same position and draw it sideways, they will make a very thin line. Keeping the felt parallel to the top of the page, pull the clamp in various circular directions to show how the line can go gradually from thick to thin.

This project is very experimental. You might suggest that the students practice making the letters of their names, but keep it very free. (It would be

↓
pull

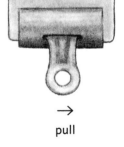

→
pull

great to draw letters of various alphabets—Arabic, Hebrew, Chinese, and so forth—especially if they are studying any of these cultures in other classes.) You will probably want several sheets of paper per student. You can use regular 12″ by 18″ paper of some sort or even large sheets of newspaper that are predominantly print. Another approach would be to unroll several feet of three-foot-wide white or butcher paper and simply let the kids have fun.

Lesson 25:   File and Free

See First Year, Lesson 13.

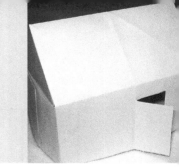

Unit Six: **Form**

Because form is so closely related to shape, and because, like line, there is not a great deal of esoteric terminology involved, this unit is also very short.

Lesson 26:   **Review of Form and Paper Houses**

Lesson Summary: Students will fold and color paper to make model houses.

Purpose: Children will learn how to fold a useful form and make it attractive from all sides.

Materials: 12″ × 18″ white construction paper (preferably made square), scissors, crayons and/or markers, staples, glue stick, or tape

Review: Elements, form (definition), dimensions, geometric, organic, irregular

Time: One period

Possible Visual Aids: Frank Lloyd Wright houses with and without flat roofs, Northwest Coast Indian longhouses

Begin by reviewing the material on form you covered in the first-year curriculum. Discuss elements in general, the definition of form in particular, how it relates to shape, what the dimensions are, organic forms, geometric forms, irregular forms, and so forth. Sculptors and architects are among the artists who deal with form, and one important aspect of their work is that they must make every side of their product interesting. The viewer should want to see all the sides, and they should all be satisfying.

This project reinforces the concept that artists need to consider all sides of a form. You may use a square or a rectangular piece of paper, but a square works better. I suggest you have your students create squares from 12″ by 18″ white construction paper, using the technique described in Lesson 42 of the first year. They should then fold with you as you do the demo.

Fold the paper in half hamburger or hot dog fold. If the paper is square, there is no difference. Open the page, turn the fold vertically, and fold one of the parallel edges to the center fold. Then fold the other edge to the center

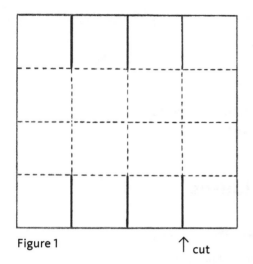

Figure 1   ↑ cut

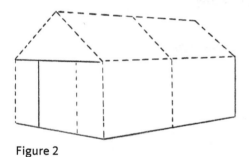

Figure 2

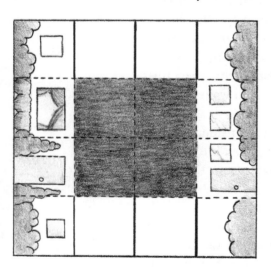

fold as well. Open the paper, and fold it in half horizontally. Fold the top and bottom edges to the middle. You should have 16 squares (or rectangles, if you didn't square the page). All the mountains should be on the same side of the page.

Cut slits according to diagram in Figure 1. This will result in four flaps on two opposing sides. Bring the two center flaps on one end together and rotate them toward each other until they completely overlap. This forms the roof of the house. Rotate the remaining two flaps on that end toward each other until they form the walls of the house. They should overlap somewhat and remain outside the roof flaps. Repeat this on the other edge. Do not secure the form in any way at this point. You are simply showing the students how the house will take form. (See diagram in Figure 2.)

On the board, draw a large square and divide it into 16 squares to reflect your folded paper. Draw it in the same position as the first diagram, with the darker slits running up the sides and the uncut strips at the top and bottom. Fill in the center four squares and explain that this will be the roof. If they want to draw some sort of shingles, depending on the design, they might need to think about the direction of those shingles. If they color the roof solidly, the direction will not matter.

The bottom center two uncut squares represent the front of the house and the two ends will wrap around to form part of the sides. You could show how to cut a door or windows, and draw in shrubbery, flowers, porch lights, and so forth. Keep everything on this bottom strip running in the same direction. They will then turn the piece around and draw the back of the house on the opposite two center squares. It is best to put only bushes on the end squares that wrap around, but if a student can envision where windows will end up, they can certainly include these as well. It is also a good idea to leave the two center flaps on each side, the ones that will completely overlap, totally blank. The children can use markers or crayons.

Once the coloring is complete, you may glue, tape, or staple the house so that it retains its form. The rectangle left over from creating the square can be used to make a garage or a chimney or doghouse.

This lesson can be adapted in a number of ways. I usually let the students be as fanciful as they wish; but if your class is studying communities, for instance, you

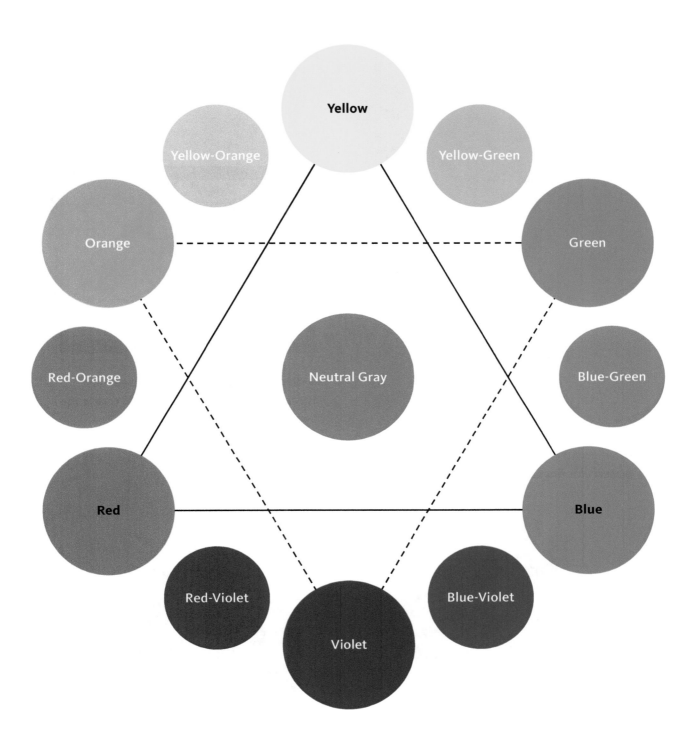

A very basic color wheel.

◀ **Creating tertiaries in fall trees.**

▲ **Second grader John Moore used only three primary-colored crayons to create the various hues in this project.**

Watercolor fingerprints ▼

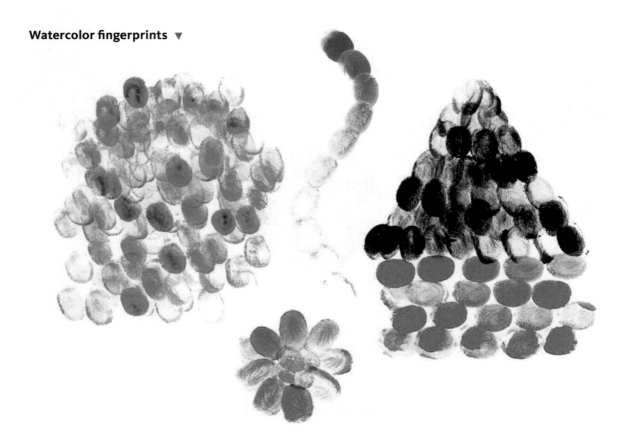

◄ Second grader John Khantsis's anteater is split into four different color schemes.

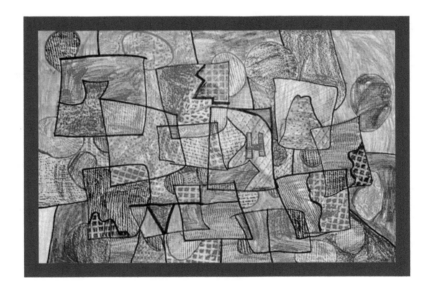

► First graders Nytalia Patterson and Alexander Dall created these very different compositions filled with texture.

**Second graders Meena Moorthy and Anne Havlik mixed primaries
and secondaries to create these terrific colors.**

Anne Havlik created this excellent distortion project.

Third graders Grace DeBrota, Ben Klemz, Elenna Cuevas, and Peter Steinbart solved this informal balance

problem using monochromatic, complementary, triadic, and analogous color schemes, respectively.

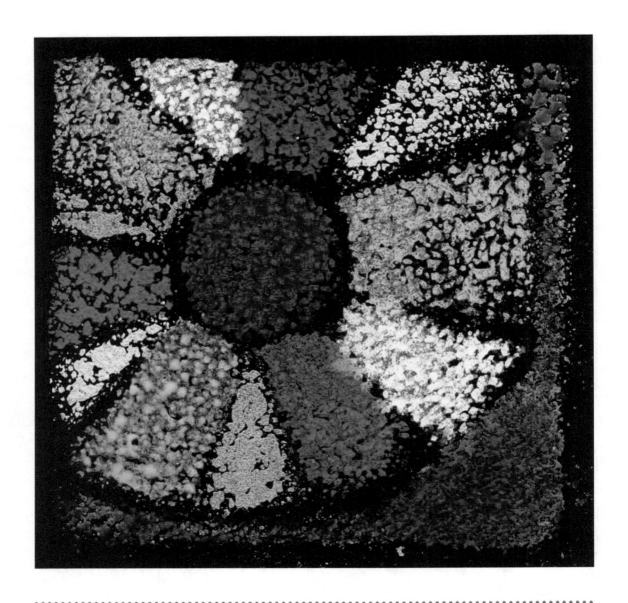

The texture for the unity project should look something like this.

could have children create different kinds of buildings you have discussed. The form could also be adapted to the communal houses of the Northwest Coast Indians. The leftover piece could be made into a cylinder to represent the totem pole at the entrance. Older students could really elaborate on this basic form, or you could use another form entirely. There are myriad folded forms associated with geometry that make beautiful sculptures. For example, Bradford Hansen Smith has a Web site, www.wholemovement.com, and books that show how paper plates can be used to create incredible results.

Lesson 27: Organic Form Sculpture

Lesson Summary: Students will create a sculpture that displays organic form.

Purpose: The lesson will reinforce the concept of organic form and give the students experience in sculpture.

Materials: Wood blocks, approximately 3″ or 4″ on a side and 1″-thick nylon hose, wire, approximately 3′ per student (a thin coat hanger with the twist cut off is fine), tempera paint mixed with white glue, hot glue (optional), twist ties, rubber bands, or string (optional)

Review: Form (definition), geometric, organic, irregular, sculpture

Time: Two periods

Possible Visual Aids: Works of Henry Moore

I must admit I have never tried this project, although I know people who have done it successfully with young children. My schedule has never allowed enough time, but if you can work it in, I recommend it. Different people have been credited with starting this lesson. To see the general idea, put "nylon stocking sculpture" into your Internet search engine and study the various results.

After reviewing form—geometric, organic, and irregular—you can demonstrate the project. You will need a thick wood block about three inches square, although any scrap pieces that are large enough will do. For younger children, this should be pre-drilled with two holes that match the size of the wire you use. Coat hangers are certainly the cheapest source of wire, but I would use the thinner ones. If you use coat hangers, cut them on each arm near the twist and open them out, so that the students have a simple, relatively straight piece of wire to work with. They will simply bend the piece into an interesting form and insert the two ends into the holes in the wood. The tension should keep them secure, but if your holes are too large, you might want to apply some hot glue.

Each student will place a nylon stocking over the wire and secure at the base. Knee-highs would probably be great, and you could start asking for these and stockpiling them early in the year. For young students, you could secure the bottom with a large twist tie, string, rubber band, or yarn and then have them trim off the excess. Or you could apply a little hot glue to keep the nylon in place. Finally, you could mix some thinned white glue with tempera and let them paint the sculpture, or use the various approaches suggested on the Internet.

After your review and demonstration, which need not include the painting step unless you are prepping the nylon in some way, simply pass out the materials and begin.

Lesson 28: **Contrast and Compare**

Lesson Summary: Students will contrast and compare works of art.

Purpose: Students will observe how artists use elements and principles to express themselves.

Materials: Works of art, real or reproductions

Review: (In the course of the discussion) element, color, shape, texture, value, line, form, illusion, movement, balance, contrast, compare (many others, depending on the images)

Possible Visual Aids: Possibly N. C. Wyeth's *Blue Lock, The Queen;* Wassily Kandinsky's *Lyric (Man on a Horse);* Koryusai's *Winter;* Romare Bearden's *She-Ba;* or Robert Reid's *The White Parasol*

Read Lesson 45 of the first year. This exercise is essentially the same, you are simply using different images. You might try comparing N. C. Wyeth's *Blue Lock, The Queen* with Wassily Kandinsky's *Lyric (Man on a Horse).* Or you might add a third piece, choosing Koryusai's *Winter,* Romare Bearden's *She-Ba,* and Robert Reid's *The White Parasol.*

Third Year

THE THIRD-YEAR CURRICULUM focuses on the principles of art, specifically balance, emphasis, distortion, contrast, unity, movement, and rhythm. We don't do projects that center around pattern, overlap, repetition, or other principles that were covered at length in previous years, although we refer to that vocabulary frequently.

Since the principles refer to how an artist uses the elements, it is important to review those concepts, especially terms used in color theory, because several of the projects will require a color scheme. Thus, our year begins with an extensive review of color and value vocabulary, followed by a test. Any necessary review of shape, line, texture, or form will be woven into the various projects, but if you prefer, you could go over this terminology as well. I am including a test I use for review in grade eight that covers all of the elements and principles, but I only use questions 1 through 21 in grade three. If you are condensing the three years of curriculum into one (or less), you might give this part of the test plus questions 22, 23, 33, 34, 35, 36, 37, and 38, before you move on from elements to principles, or simply use the whole instrument at the end of the year. If you are not condensing the material, this review will help not only returning students, but children new to the material.

Each third grade project takes several periods. Always start a period with a brief review of the concepts and instructions.

Name: _____

1. Another word for the name of a color is _____.

2. Three properties of color are _____ , _____ , and _____.

3. The primary colors are _____ , _____ , and _____.

4. How do you make green? _____
   _____

5. How do you make an intermediate color? _____
   _____
   _____

6. Give two examples of intermediate colors. _____
   _____

7. Give two reasons why primary colors are important. _____
   _____
   _____

8. White added to a color makes a _____.

9. Black added to a color makes a _____.

10. _____ refers to lightness and darkness.

11. The brightness or dullness of a color is its _____.

12. If you mix two primary colors together equally, you get a _____ color.

13. If you take all the light away, you will see _____.

14. If sunlight hits an object and none of the light is absorbed, it all bounces back to hit your eye.

    You will see that object as _____.

15. If I add a little of its opposite to a color, I will _____ the color.

16. If I mix opposite colors equally, I will get _____.

17. If I put two opposite colors side by side, they _____.

18. Another word for opposite colors is _____.

19. The secondary colors form a _____ color scheme.

20. If I use mostly red, maroon, pink, rose, brick red, black, white, and gray to make a painting,

I have used a _____ color scheme.

21. Related colors lying next to each other on the color wheel form an _____

_____ color scheme.

22. Texture is _____

_____

23. Define form.

_____

_____

_____

24. Name three general types of BALANCE. _____ , _____ ,

and _____ .

25. What type of balance is exhibited by example   a. _____

b. _____   c. _____

26. Repetition of a motif creates _____ .

27. A sense of oneness, or wholeness, in a work of art is _____ .

28. Using an element of art more than once is referred to as _____ .

29. _____ is another word for "difference" in an artwork.

30. _____ is the principle of design by which the artist draws special

attention to a particular area, object, feeling, or idea.

31. _____ is achieved when a subject is pulled "out of shape" in some way

but is still recognizable.

32. _____ refers to how the viewer's eye is directed through the work of art.

33. Define "line" as it applies to art. _____

_____

_____

34. In what way(s) does a "line" in art differ from one in math? _____

_____

_____

35. In what way do "calligraphic" lines differ from "contour" lines?

_____

_____

_____

36. Define "shape." _____

_____

_____

37. In the following picture, how would you refer to the X shapes versus the Y shapes?

The X shapes are _____. The Y shapes are _____.

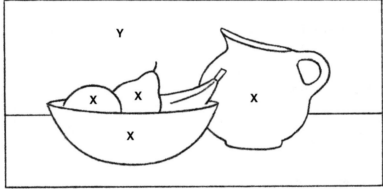

38. Shapes A, B, and C are all _____.

Shape D is _____.

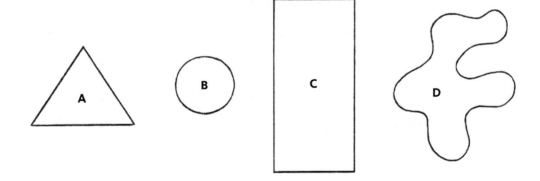

Lesson 1: Creating a Portfolio

See Lesson 1 of the First and Second Years.

Lesson 2: Review of Color and Value Vocabulary

Lesson Summary: The class will review color and value vocabulary and take a test.

Purpose: The lesson will reinforce students' understanding of color theory and physics of light before they move on to the study of principles.

Answer key for puzzle:
4A hue; 5A warm; 8A tint; 9A cool; 10A intermediate; 11A shade; 12A primary: 14A white; 15A dull; 16A black; 17A glow; 18A tertiary; 19A monochromatic; 20A black or gray; 1D secondary; 2D value; 3D triadic; 6D intensity; 7D complementary; 13D analogous. Back: Two reasons primaries are important: 1 They can be mixed to make all the other colors. 2 No other colors can be mixed to make them. Three ways to describe a color: 1 hue; 2 value; 3 intensity. You make a secondary color by mixing two primary colors evenly. One way to make an intermediate is to mix two primaries unevenly.

Answer Key for Test:
1. hue 2. hue, value, intensity 3. red, yellow, and blue (I give extra credit for knowing the primary colors of light: red, blue, and green) 4. mix blue and yellow evenly 5. (possible extra credit if two answers are given) mix two primary colors unevenly or mix a primary with a nonopposite secondary or mix two colors next two each other on the color wheel 6. blue-green, yellow-orange, green-blue, etc. 7. they can be mixed to make any other color but no other colors can be mixed to make them 8. tint 9. shade 10. value 11. intensity 12. secondary 13. black 14. white 15. dull 16. black 17. glow (get brighter, intensify each other, etc.) 18. complementary 19. triadic 20. monochromatic 21. analogous 22. The way something feels or appears to feel 23. a three-dimensional, closed figure 24. formal, radial, informal 25. (For this question, you will need three visual aids, one that demonstrates symmetry, one that demonstrates informal balance, and one that shows radial balance.) 26. pattern 27. unity 28. repetition 29. contrast 30. emphasis 31. distortion 32. movement 33. the path of a moving point 34. a line in math has only one dimension, while a line in art might have two or even three; also, a line in art can get thicker or thinner 35. calligraphic lines get thicker and thinner, while

During this review, the students will be making a color wheel. Depending on the age of your pupils, you might copy the simple diagram I have included, or you might have your class create something more sophisticated. We use crayon in this lesson, but you could certainly use paint for a more accurate result. The crossword puzzle is also geared to a younger child, but it can work for older students as well. You might simply go over the color and value vocabulary rather quickly and give the test, but I would strongly recommend doing a color wheel at some point. If you are condensing this book's curriculum for an older age group, you could start with physics of light and why we see black and white. Then you could make a color wheel and work your way from primary to secondary to intermediate color-mixing lessons and finish with color schemes. This lesson describes the procedure I use in grade three. If you are not fluent in color theory, you will probably want to look at the earlier chapters on color and value before you begin.

On the back of the crossword puzzle, I add these additional questions: "Two reasons why primary colors are important are..." "Three ways to define or describe color are..." "How do you make a secondary color?" and "One way to make an intermediate is... (See 10 Across for the other way.)"

Give each child a copy of the color-wheel diagram and the crossword puzzle and have them put their names on both. These are the sheets they will study for the test, so it is important that they be filled in accurately. We work the puzzle generally in the order that the concepts were introduced in the first two years, so we don't necessarily go in the exact order of the questions as presented. The students supply the answers, and I illustrate concepts such as "tint," "shade," or "intermediates" using paint. Whenever I elicit a response, I write the number and answer on the board, such as "4A—Hue."

A little of this material will be new. The answers to 5 and 9 Across could be analogous, but the four-letter answers we are seeking are "warm" and "cool," respectively. The curriculum has not really explored this concept as such, so you could spend some time discussing it here.

When you reach 12 Across, "Red, yellow, and blue are _____ colors," have the students begin filling in their color wheels. If you use crayon for the

The Color Wheel

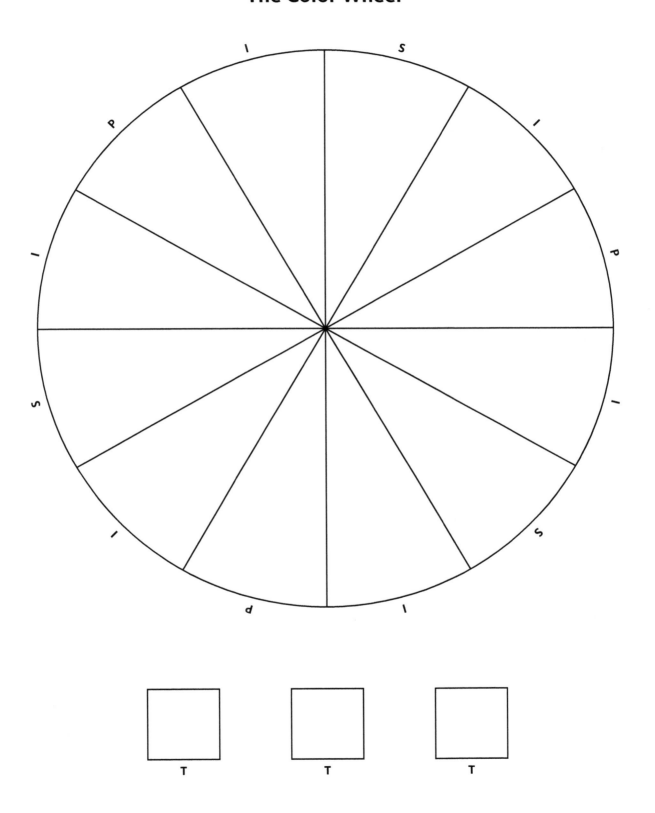

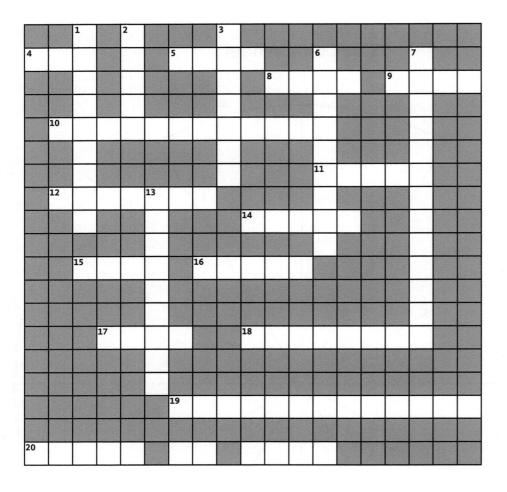

ACROSS

4. Another word for color is _____ .

5. Yellow, orange, and red are _____ colors.

8. White added to a color makes a _____ .

9. Blue, green, and violet are _____ colors.

10. One way to make this kind of color is to mix a primary with a secondary next to it on the color wheel.

11. Black added to a color makes a _____ .

12. Red, yellow, and blue are _____ colors.

14. If sunlight hits an object and none of it is absorbed, it all bounces back to hit my eye. I will see the object as _____ .

15. A little of a color added to its opposite will _____ it.

16. If you take all the light away, you will see _____ .

17. If I put two opposite colors side by side, they will _____ .

18. If I mix two secondary colors, I will get a _____ .

19. A color scheme that uses different tints, shades, and intensities of only one color is called _____ .

20. If I mix equal amounts of two opposites, I will get _____ .

DOWN

1. Orange, green, and violet are _____ colors.

2. _____ refers to lightness and darkness.

3. The secondary colors form a _____ color scheme.

6. _____ refers to the brightness or dullness of a color.

7. Colors opposite each other on the color wheel are _____ .

13. _____ colors are related and lie next to each other on the color wheel.

wheel, make sure your students use true red, yellow, and blue. Draw a replica color wheel on the board (if you have a whiteboard) or on a large piece of paper. Point out the letters around the edge, and ask what the *P*s stand for. By now, everyone should guess "primary." Explain that any primary can go in any *P* section. They might put red at the bottom *or* yellow *or* blue. The only thing that matters is that they fill only the sections marked *P*. These three sections are equally far apart. All color wheels start with the three primary colors placed equally far apart.

When you reach 1 Down, ask what the *S* on the wheel stands for, and have the students fill the *S* sections with the secondary colors from their crayon boxes. If they are using paint or some other mixable medium, they should mix two primaries and place the resulting secondary *between those two*. (Be aware that color-wheel red and blue make a pretty muddy purple. Magenta works better, but it is not the red we find on the wheel.) Technically, once you lay down the primaries, the rest of the wheel is created by mixing equal amounts of two adjacent colors and placing the result halfway between the two. Unfortunately, this rarely yields perfect results and the artist has to tinker a little. *The important thing is that orange should lie halfway between red and yellow, green should lie halfway between blue and yellow, and purple, or violet, should lie halfway between red and blue.*

When you begin discussing intermediates, have students mix for those colors regardless of the medium. If you are using crayon, have pupils fill an *I* slot with a fairly heavy layer of the lighter of the two hues that border it, then lay the other color on top until the result looks about halfway between the two. Thus, if they are filling the space that lies between yellow and orange, they will put the yellow down first and layer orange on top of it until the section appears to be a medium orange-yellow/yellow-orange. Make sure they are mixing in the *I* sections.

Of course, the *T* boxes at the bottom of the color wheel page are for mixing tertiary colors. Whatever medium you are using, simply have the students mix a different pair of secondaries in each box. If you are using crayon, put the lighter hue in first, pressing a little more firmly.

Don't forget to discuss and fill in the questions on the back of the crossword puzzle. When both sheets are complete, you might actually read the test in class as a question and answer practice to make sure you have not forgotten anything, then simply give the test during the next art period.

There is an interesting question you might ask your students when you review complementary colors. Why are the walls of many operating rooms painted green? The answer is included in the answer key at the end of the gray box.

Lesson 3: Introducing Balance, Formal Balance, and Symmetry

Balance: Even distribution of weight
Formal Balance: Balance of similar things on each side of a center line
Symmetry: Balance of identical things on each side of a center line

Lesson Summary: Students will create a symmetrical picture or design using simple materials.

Purpose: Students will study symmetry and formal balance. The project will reinforce the concept of symmetry.

Materials: 9″ × 12″ white construction paper, chalk, crayons, pencils, manila paper, magazines (optional)

Review: Balance, symmetry

New Vocabulary/Concept: Formal balance

Time: Five to six periods

Possible Visual Aid: Chinese Tao' T'ieh

As you will see, this unit presents some wonderful opportunities to integrate art with science and math. It is a good idea to begin with a brief discussion of the difference between elements and principles, so you might want to review the pertinent material from Lesson 24 of the first year. Explain that the class is going to be focusing on principles rather than elements this year and that the first principle they will cover will be balance. Ask if anyone can define balance, and elicit or provide the information that it refers to the even distribution of weight. If I am standing on one foot, in order to balance, I must distribute my weight differently than I do when standing on two feet. You might, of course, discuss other uses of the word, such as balanced reporting, or a bank balance.

Different elements create weight in a work of art—colors, shapes, lines, values, textures, and forms all draw the eye to different parts of the composition in different ways and affect its balance. In a sculpture, the term might be used both visually and literally. There are several ways to visually balance works of art, and one easy way to discuss them is to create an analogy with playground equipment. You might ask students what apparatus at a park requires weight to be distributed evenly in order to work efficiently. While several answers might be somewhat true, try to elicit the concept of a teeter-totter.

Draw a simple diagram on the board: a straight line over a triangular fulcrum in the center. Ask what kind of simple machine a teeter-totter is. They should know it is a lever. Then you might say something like the following.

"Let's say you weigh 50 pounds." Draw a simple shape on one end of the seesaw and put a "50" inside. "You are on one end of the teeter-totter and you want to have a great 'teeter' with someone. What size person should you invite to play with you? That's right, a 50-pound person. And that person should sit equally far from the fulcrum."

Draw a similar shape at the other end of the teeter-totter and place a "50" inside it as well. "If you both sit very still, the seesaw should balance in a perfectly horizontal line, and you should have no trouble going up and down.

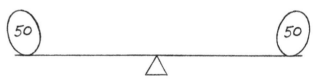

"Now let's say you and the person at the other end are identical twins. You look exactly alike and are wearing the same clothes. You are sitting equally far from the center and you are facing each other. This type of balance is called symmetry. We've talked about symmetry before. A butterfly's wings are bilaterally symmetrical, and so are people. Symmetry is the balance of identical things on each side of a center line. One side appears to be a mirror image of the other.

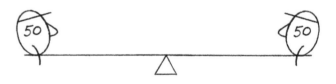

"Now let's say that the fulcrum remains in the center of the teeter-totter, but the 50-pound person on the other end doesn't look anything like you. One of you is a boy and one is a girl. One of you is wearing a baseball cap and shorts. The other is wearing jeans. One is facing the middle and the other is facing away. But each of you has a total weight of 50 pounds and you are equally far from the fulcrum. Will the teeter-totter still balance?"

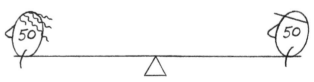

(You'll be surprised by the number of young children who answer "no.") "Of course it will! The teeter-totter doesn't care what you look like—it only cares how much you weigh. This is an example of formal balance. Formal balance is the balance of like things on either side of a center line." Draw simple images of trees like these shown and discuss the differences and similarities. "All symmetry is formal balance, but not all formal balance is symmetrical. You could say that symmetry is the most exact kind of formal balance."

Explain that some people use the two terms interchangeably, that is, they will call generally formal compositions, like *Christ Giving the Keys (of Paradise) to St. Peter* by Perugino, symmetrical, when it is only very formal. A Chinese Tao' T'ieh figure, on the other hand, is perfectly symmetrical and makes a

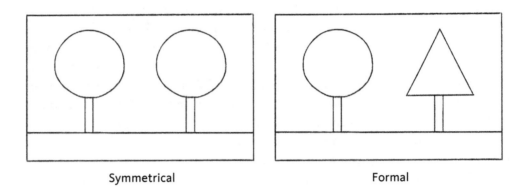

| Symmetrical | Formal |

great visual aid for this lesson, because the project for this concept is going to demonstrate symmetry, not just formal balance.

This task requires chalk, crayons, pencils, and paper. You should also have some magazines or newspaper for padding.

I use 9" by 12" construction paper, but regular computer paper will work as well. For your demonstration, fold the paper carefully in half. Hot dog folds create more compositional challenges than hamburger folds, but either is fine. In third grade, we use only hamburger folds. You now have a little booklet. Place your name in a corner on the outside. It is very important to put your name on the page before you begin the project. Next, open the fold and turn the top half back and under so that only one half of the paper shows. Once again you have a little booklet, but now your name is on the inside. Place the booklet on a magazine. (Working on a magazine or other padded surface sometimes makes applying the chalk and crayon easier, but cover the magazine so that the print doesn't come off onto the clean side of the project that is folded under. I use a 9" by 12" piece of manila for this.) Cover the part facing up with a solid layer of chalkboard chalk. We use white chalk so that nothing detracts from the symmetry of the finished piece, but be aware that this makes it very difficult to see places you have missed. You will have to hold the piece up to the light at different angles to be sure it is totally covered. Any color chalk will do, so you might want to use yellow or some other pale tone. Make sure that your hand does not brush off the chalk as you work.

Choose a very dark value crayon like black or violet-blue. Cover the layer of chalk completely with a layer of crayon. Try not to remove chalk as you do this. If you press too hard with the crayon, you will push up little mounds of chalk dust that will cause flaking. If you used white chalk, be sure you are crayoning the side with the chalk and not the clean half of the page. The crayon should ultimately be very dark and solid.

Open the booklet. The side of the paper with your name should have nothing else on it, and the other side should be half blank and half colored. Fold the blank half back up and over the chalk/crayon half as it was when you first put your name on the project. (The crayon is now inside the booklet.) With a sharp pencil, draw a design on the outside of the folded page, being sure to draw solid shapes filled in with pencil, or wide lines. Discuss positive and negative shape. Explain that lots of small shapes with a large negative space will not work well for this project. Urge them not to make little bitty details. Keep the piece on a magazine as you work. Be sure to place the fold of the paper vertically, not across the top or bottom. (Please note, you cannot shade or erase the pencil marks. Shapes are either black or white.) Do not use too sharp a pencil or go over your marks too heavily. The crayon should not only transfer to the white half of the interior of piece, but if you have chalked correctly, it will "lift" completely off the dark side, creating a symmetrical result that emphasizes positive and negative shape.

Third grader Moira Kelly created this striking symmetrical composition.

If you must store the project before or after it is done, close the booklet in such a way that the crayon/chalk half is on the inside. Place a 6″ by 9″ piece of manila (or 4½″ by 12″ piece if you made a hot dog fold) inside to protect the project. Be sure students never draw on the project while this protector sheet is inside.

Lesson 4: Radial Balance

Balance around, toward, or away from a center point

Lesson Summary: Students create an umbrella design in crayon resist.

Purpose: Students will explore the concept of radial balance and use it in the project.

Materials: 9″ × 12″ construction paper, preprinted with an octagon, scissors, pencils, crayons, black watercolor paint, brushes, water buckets, paper towels, 12″ × 18″ manila (optional)

Review: Balance, symmetry, formal, color schemes, crayon resist

New Vocabulary/Concept: Radial balance

Time: Six to seven periods

Possible Visual Aids: Certain Native American pots and woven baskets

After a brief review of formal balance and symmetry, introduce the word "radial," and ask if anyone knows what it means. Ask for other words with the same root. Discuss things like a radial tire, radiator, radio (the sound radiates), radius, and so forth. Then ask, "What piece of playground equipment seems related to this concept?" Some children might suggest a tire swing, which is true in some cases, but you are trying to elicit the idea of a merry-go-round. Draw a simple bird's-eye view of one and ask, "If you go to the playground with some friends and want to have a long ride, where should you jump on?" They will all know that everyone should not board the apparatus on the same side—they should spread themselves evenly around the edge. If possible,

explain a little about the mechanics of the merry-go-round. Remind them that balance refers to the even distribution of weight. Discuss the fact that not all of the children on the playground will weigh the same amount, so they must arrange themselves somewhat randomly.

A great example of radial balance is a spiral. You could also make simple drawings on the board of things like round table saw blades, bike spokes, and so forth. These are figures that are not technically symmetrical, but they are radial. Some radial designs are symmetrical as well, but it is not necessary. Hubcaps are a great source of radial designs. (In fact, you might have older students design hubcaps as their final projects.) You could also discuss examples of radial balance in biology or botany.

We define radial balance as "the even distribution of weight around, toward, or away from a center point." The key issue is that the balance radiates from a point. There is no line of symmetry required.

After discussing the idea of radial balance, introduce the project. Create a diagram like the one shown. Enlarge it (ours measure about 8¼″ from one point to its diametric opposite), and copy it onto construction paper, if possible. If not, regular copy paper will do. Explain to the students that they are going to design an umbrella. The lines represent the struts. They will cut out the octagonal shape and put their name on the side that has the lines. This is the back of the project. A student will probably be able to see the lines through the paper when she lays it on her desk, but if not, she can hold it up to the light and find the center. This point should be drawn on the front. If you are dealing with older students, this would be a great opportunity to integrate even more mathematics by having them construct their own octagon. The design should be drawn *very lightly* with pencil. Remind students that umbrellas have no up or down. I can twirl an umbrella as I walk, and it will always look right-side up to a person behind me. This is the ultimate test of their design. No matter which way they turn the octagon, the design should look balanced. Warn them not to start with squares or triangles in the center. While these can be made to work, it is difficult and can result in shapes that are too small for this project. If a student uses a spiral, you might suggest that they start from the outside and work their way in. This helps keep the spiral round. Try to avoid designs that are more symmetrical than radial.

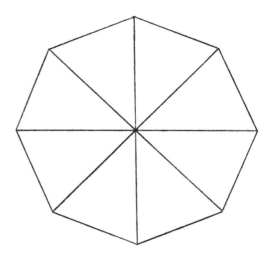

There are two factors that must be considered: the design must be radial and it must be balanced. If a student covered his umbrella with a checkerboard, that would be very balanced but not radial. If the design looked like daisy petals growing from the center, but there were three very fat petals on one side and the rest were thin, that would be radial but not balanced. Be sure the children understand the requirements.

This project is going to be completed in crayon resist, so none of the shapes should be too small to carry a heavy layer of crayon. Have the students select a color scheme. If they have used lines in their designs, they should color right next to the line rather than on top of it. This will produce a cleaner effect. If they are using filled-in areas, they should leave a small space between adjacent shapes. The general rule in this project is "Stay off the pencil lines." Make sure the crayon is very waxy. When the crayoning is complete, paint over the entire surface with black watercolor. Make sure the paint is rich enough to dry a true black, but not so "sticky" thick that it covers the crayon. We place each octagon on a piece of 12″ by 18″ manila while painting and then leave it on the manila when placing it on the drying rack.

This project can be very simple or extremely complicated. Three thin lines that create concentric circles in red, yellow, and blue on a mostly black background will solve the problem correctly if not uniquely. Some students will produce incredibly involved geometric patterns that cover the entire area with color.

Each year, our parent-teacher association holds an auction as a fundraiser. Parents of third graders may bid on the chance to have their child's radial design painted on a real umbrella. I do the painting, using a black umbrella and acrylic paint. These can be used in the rain, and they are quite lovely.

Lesson 5: Informal Balance

Balance of unlike things on each side of a center line

Lesson Summary: The children will create a project using dripped paint and colored media.

Purpose: The students will learn about and practice informal balance.

Materials: 12″ × 18″ white construction paper, watered-down black tempera paint in squeeze bottles, pencils, crayons, markers, colored pencils, sponges, paper towels, sponge buckets (optional), plastic or rubber gloves (optional), smocks (optional, but recommended)

Review: Balance, formal, symmetry, radial, color scheme, shape, gradation

New Vocabulary/Concept: Informal balance

After reviewing formal and radial balance, go back to the analogy of the teeter-totter and discuss alternative ways in which you might have a good time on the apparatus even if the person you are playing with is much heavier or lighter. "If Mom takes you to the park, how can you have a great teeter even though she's twice your weight?" The students will probably know that the heavier person needs to move closer to the fulcrum. (Physics in action!) Placement of shapes depending on the size or color can greatly affect balance in a work of art, and that placement need not be formal. Illustrate this with a simple drawing.

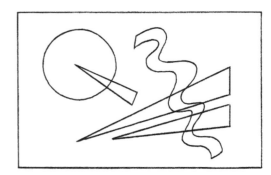

Another possibility is to add more weight to one side until it equals the other, another nice way to incorporate math and science. For example, two 30-pound children at one end will balance a 60-pound child at the other. We actually imagine some pretty silly scenarios: one 30-pound child plus 30 one-pound children equals... We come up with several equations that are accurate, if impossible.

I would guess that most works of art throughout history have been informally balanced, so producing visual aids should not be an issue. Creating symmetry with the project for this unit would be almost impossible, so once students begin, you need only focus on whether the piece is balanced and has appropriate negative spaces. The first step is extremely messy, so you will want to take some precautions.

This project is a variation on the one where the student applies and blows on paint using a straw. I like this approach much better, because the artist has greater control and there is less likelihood that a student will pass out or inhale paint.

Begin by watering down a quantity of black tempera. The paint should be thin enough to drip freely, but it should dry black, not gray. I use a large plastic pitcher that can be sealed. Hopefully, you will have some empty pint tempera squeeze bottles, but if not, plastic catsup or mustard containers should work. If the empty tempera bottles contained something other than black, rinse them thoroughly before filling them one-third to one-half full of the diluted black tempera. Practice the following steps until you are comfortable with the results before doing the demonstration.

Place a piece of 12″ by 18″ white construction paper on the table. Carefully place several drops of the black tempera in random places over the surface.

Start with 8 to 10 drops. These should be drops, not puddles—maybe one-half to one centimeter in diameter. Do not squeeze the bottle. Turn it gently until it starts to drip. Caution the students to do this slowly.

Pick the paper up by pinching one edge between the thumb and forefinger of *one* hand. Shake gently but firmly until the paint runs in lines. You can control this run to a certain extent. If you want the paint to run diagonally, hold the paper in a corner. You can even make the paint create circular lines by rotating the page. The important thing to do now is to create shapes. Remember, a shape is a flat, *closed* figure. If your lines are mostly vertical, cross them with horizontal lines and vice versa. Do not overdo the paint—you don't want a black page with tiny white spaces, although even that result can be effective. Continue adding drops and creating lines until you have a solid composition. When you do the demo, you don't need to fill the whole page, just give students the idea.

Although the class is going to add color to the project, I don't discuss that until each child has a basic black and white design to work with. When setting up, I have each student share a paint bottle with the person across from him or her. Smocks are a good idea, but if you are using an old shirt, be careful that sleeves don't drag across the wet project. Place paint and pencils on the table, pass out paper, and be sure the children put their names on the backs of the pages before they begin. Once they start, the paper cannot be turned over and you don't want them touching the front. When all the names are written, remove the pencils from the tables and show the students where fresh paper can be accessed, putting a pencil nearby. Students will have wildly different time frames for this project, and they should create as many designs as time allows. I usually set aside three to four periods for this step, hoping that each child will have at least two results to choose from. Some will have four or five. Be aware that problems can occur. Students can drop the paper face down, and if the paint smears they will have to start over. Also, caution them to avoid putting their fingers in the paint at the edges of the paper when they grasp it. The design should tessellate the page.

When the children shake the page, a great deal of paint may end up on the tables. (Be sure they don't shake over the floor!) It is a good idea to circulate with a slightly damp sponge and wipe up large drips so that the backs of the papers don't get too full of paint. Don't make the tables wet—just wipe off puddles. If you have adult help—an assistant, team teacher, or parent—give them sponges as well. Also, it's a great idea to wear plastic or rubber gloves while doing cleanup duty.

When a student finishes a design, they simply place it on the drying rack and start another. Be sure any new piece has a name on it. Even though children will have very different styles, it will be extremely hard to recognize one's own paper a few days later. Check the work to make sure there are plenty of shapes and that the piece looks balanced. Stop work a little early each period, because cleaning the desks will take some time. I have students remove the paint bottles and take a bucket of sponges to each table. Each child is responsible for his or her own desk. They will need to rinse and wring sponges in the sink before the job is done.

Once everyone has a good result to work from, discuss coloring. I use my original demos to show how colors may be added. Students may use crayon, marker, and/or colored pencil. Once again, they must select a color scheme. Some people will color every single shape, while others will fill in only a few. A lot depends on the black and white design. Even though the paint is dry, do not color over it, especially with marker. It will smear into the colored medium and make it look dirty. Do not allow students to use black crayon, marker, or colored pencil, although gray is fine. Be very careful about balance, as informal balance is the point of the project. Warn the children that they

Third graders Grace DeBrota, Ben Klemz, Elenna Cuevas, and Peter Steinbart solved informal balance problems in their works. (See color insert)

cannot suddenly introduce a new color three-fourths of the way across the page, or use all their light or bright colors on one side only. It will also throw the balance off if they use marker on one side and light crayon on the other. If they fill a relatively large shape on one side with a color, it may be necessary to fill several small adjacent shapes on the other side with that color to balance it. There are many factors to consider, and you should remind them that "art is constant decision making!" Encourage them to start coloring in the center and spiral outward. If they must color in an area that is not quite closed, they should not draw a sharp line across the opening—it will not go with the style of the drips. Use crayon or colored pencil and fade out at the opening. In fact gradation can create wonderful effects on this project. Whatever creative approach a student chooses, make sure they balance it throughout the work. If they decide to put polka-dots in a space, they need to repeat that approach in other areas.

Lesson 6:　Emphasis Through Distortion and Contrast

Stressing or calling attention to something

Lesson Summary: Students will trace their hands and feet to create distorted cartoon figures.

Purpose: Students will learn about emphasis. The project will create emphasis through the use of distortion and contrast.

Materials: 18″ × 24″ white construction paper (preferable), pencils, multicultural markers, multicultural crayons, markers, crayons

Review: Principles, distortion, repetition, contrast

New Vocabulary/Concepts: Emphasis, melanin (optional)

Time: Approximately 15 periods (This will take far less time with older children.)

Possible Visual Aids: Works by Thomas Hart Benton, especially *The Lord Is My Shepherd*, and by William Johnson

This lesson focuses on several principles, two of which the students have studied previously. The main topic of the unit is emphasis. Ask if anyone knows what this word means. You may have to use the verb form, but even younger children frequently know what it means to "emphasize" something. Use several examples. For instance, you might speak very softly then stress a word by saying it much more loudly. Explain several ways in which advertisements emphasize the product, perhaps through repetition, and so forth. When the children understand the basic meaning of the term—stressing or calling attention to something—start discussing the many ways in which the principle can be achieved in art. Draw a large rectangle on the board and fill it with five rows of five circles. Ask what is being emphasized and elicit the idea of a circle. Ask the students how that emphasis was achieved, and write "repetition" on the board. Erase one of the circles and draw it with a somewhat wobbly line. Ask what is emphasized now and how. Hopefully, they will remember "distortion" from the previous year. Elicit the concept and put the word on the board. This would be a good time to do a brief review of distortion, perhaps using some of the devices from Lesson 20 of the second year.

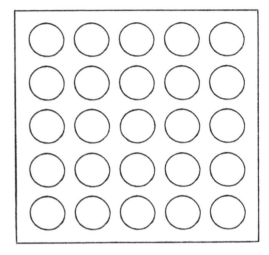

Replace the distorted circle with a regular one and fill it in with black. Ask what is being emphasized and how. Write "contrast" on the board. Ask, "What is being contrasted?" Under contrast, write "value." Erase the black interior, and fill the circle with a color, like red. Discuss the fact that this time, the emphasis was achieved through contrast of color. Erase the colored circle and replace it with a square. What is being emphasized now? How? Under contrast, add shape. Erase the square and replace the circle. "What if I cut a ball in half and glued it on this circle, or cut a piece of burlap to fit?" Add form and texture to the list under contrast. If possible, draw the circle in a different quality of line. Stress the fact that these principles apply to all the elements. An artist can repeat or contrast or distort color, shape, texture, value, line, or form. Erase all the circles and fill the rectangle with one huge shape. Size is another way of creating emphasis. Erase the big circle and draw a fairly small circle in the center of the rectangle. Draw another rectangle next to the first and place a similar circle down low in a corner. Placement creates emphasis as well. They may have heard the phrase "in your face." When someone wants you to pay attention to them, they sometimes stand very close to you.

Once the children understand that there are many ways to create emphasis, explain that they are going to use distortion and contrast as their primary methods. This project is based upon a lesson plan that appeared in *School Arts Magazine* some years ago that involves tracing hands and bare feet, so if your room is carpeted, you might need to find a place with a hard surface floor. Also, a few words about proper tracing techniques is in order. Caution the students to hold their pencils vertically, as perpendicular to the page as possible. (You might slide in the definition of "perpendicular.") If they angle their pencils under their hands, they will get a result that looks like an alien. They should press very lightly and let the pencil be guided by the form, not push against it. Tracing feet should not be a problem, but tracing the dominant hand might be. The good news is, our left and right hands are shaped the same, so if a student is right-handed, she can use her left hand for both the hands in her picture by simply tracing it palm up or palm down. In fact, depending on the pose, she might not have to flip it at all.

The trickiest part of this project is knowing where to place the hands and feet on the page. If you are uncomfortable with this, pick a few basic poses and have the children choose from among them.

Explain that they are going to create pictures of themselves. They will be using 18″ by 24″ white construction paper. (If this is too pricey, or you cannot obtain it, simply tape two 12″ by 18″ pieces together as evenly as possible.) They will be tracing their hands and feet actual size, but even with the bigger paper, this will not allow for full-sized bodies, so the image will be automatically distorted. The hands and feet will be highly realistic, but the bodies will be "cartoony." (Our eyes tend to notice things with more detail.)

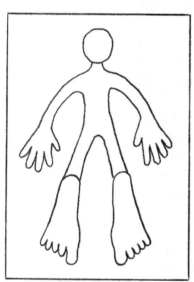 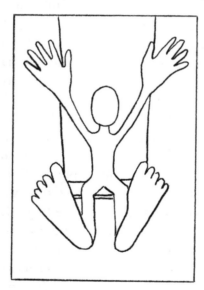

They should start by deciding on a pose. They can be doing pretty much anything in these pictures, but hands and feet will be traced flat, so you might have to think creatively. If a person is simply standing in a normal position, with his hands at his sides, the toes will be pointing down, almost touching the bottom of the page. The hands will be about halfway down the page with the fingers pointing down and the thumbs toward the center. Whenever you are checking a pose, notice where the thumbs and big toes are, and which way the fingers and toes point. Here are some basic positions.

It is a good idea to do a demonstration on the board and list the steps as well, like this: 1) Orient the paper. Explain that if the pose is essentially taller than it is wide, the paper should be turned in the portrait position, while if the pose wider than it is tall, the paper should be arranged landscape. 2) Trace the hands and feet lightly. Emphasize the word "lightly" throughout the project, because the students will probably erase a lot. 3) Draw in the body lightly. 4) Add details.

The hands and feet are going to be drawn very realistically, so you might want to point out that fingernails and toenails are not drawn with lines that go all the way across the digit. Draw something like the figure shown here on the board. Point out knuckle lines and so forth. Caution the children to think very carefully about which side of the hand or foot is showing. If a person is standing with his hands at his sides, thumbs facing in, you will see the top of the hand, while if the thumbs are facing away from the body, you will see the palms. This is also the point at which they will add faces, clothes, and so forth. 5) Add background. In most cases, this is very simple, perhaps just a line to separate the ground and sky with a few clouds.

When a student is finished with these steps, it is time to discuss coloring. We use multicultural markers and crayons for skin tones. This is a great opportunity to discuss skin color and the fact that everyone has the same pigment, melanin, and that we are all alike in this way. I speak at some length about ancestry, the protective function of the pigment, and the fact that, while people are not truly "white" or "black" or "red" or "yellow," these terms have affected our perception. A "white" person, for example, may be surprised at how dark her skin really is. Tell the students that they are to select a marker that they feel is somewhat darker than their actual skin color. It is also better to choose a crayon that is darker and press a little more lightly when that step comes. The rule for marker lines is that the thing on top gets the color. That is, if there is a line between the shirt and the pants, if the shirt is tucked in, the line will be the pant color. If the shirt is hanging out, the line will be the shirt color. A collar line will be the shirt color, while a forehead will probably get the hair color. Once again, I list the steps on the board: 1) Go over all skin lines with multicultural marker. This includes fingernails, toenails, and lips unless they have nail polish or lipstick, although anyone can use

Third graders Elizabeth Baach and Peter Steinbart drew these delightful self-portraits.

a pinker tone for lips if you have an appropriate marker. It includes knuckle and palm lines. These lines should still show after step 3. 2) Cover the rest of the pencil lines with markers. The thing on top gets the color. Check student work to make sure all pencil lines are covered before going on to crayon. 3) Fill in all skin areas with multicultural crayon. 4) Fill in rest of page with crayon and/or marker. Encourage students to use crayon somewhat lightly on large areas like sky. It will be quicker.

Lesson 7: Contrast

Difference

Lesson Summary: Students will create a project using textured paper and spray paint.

Purpose: This lesson will reinforce the concept of contrast through a project that requires the principle to succeed.

Materials: 9″ × 12″ white construction paper, pencils, scissors, black spray paint, newspapers or drop cloth, large corrugated cardboard box, straight pins, stick glue

Review: Contrast

Time: Five to six peeriods

Possible Visual Aids: Compare *Blue Poles*, by Jackson Pollack, with *Advance of History*, by Mark Tobey

This project is a favorite with the children. The more contrast the students create, the more successful the outcome will be. In addition to other materials, you will need a couple of cans of black spray paint and a ventilated area in which to spray.

Review the concept of contrast. While it has been mentioned frequently over the years, none of the lessons has focused exclusively on this principle, although it is crucial to our ability to see. A simple, one-word definition for contrast is difference. The more contrast, especially in value, the more easily we can read things. Of course, the best example is a book. We usually find black print on a white ground, not dark gray on medium gray. But the same is true in fabric or art or music or when we watch TV. Televisions still have contrast controls, which will make lights lighter and darks deeper, just like the contrast controls in PhotoShop. If a fabric is striped in dark blue on black, the pattern will not be nearly as visible as a blue stripe on yellow. You can discuss several of these examples with your students. Since I have a whiteboard, I demonstrate my point by writing the word "contrast" in yellow and in black. While the yellow is visible, the black is far easier to see.

After you have discussed various types of contrast, demonstrate the project. Start with a piece of 9″ by 12″ white construction paper. You may place it either portrait or landscape. Using a pencil, draw very light lines that divide the paper into five, six, or seven shapes. There should be no background or negative space as such. That is, the paper should be like a puzzle. None of the shapes should be particularly fragile, with small necks or easily torn arms, and of course, they should balance.

Starting in a corner of the design, cut out one of the shapes. Lay it on a corner of a second piece of 9″ by 12″ white paper, replicating its position in the original design. Trace it lightly, then put your name and the number "1" on the back. Lightly write a "1" on the tracing as well. Working your way across the page, continue to cut, trace, and label the pieces until you have duplicated the original design on the second sheet. The numbers should not jump around—that is, 2 should lie next to 3, not across the page, and the last piece should never be in the middle. Most importantly, there should be no trimming. If your scissors go off the pencil line, that will define the new shape.

Check the cut pieces and erase any pencil marks that show on the front. Then put the puzzle together, using the newly traced key. Pick up one piece and texture it. There are several ways to do this. You could crumble it, fan fold it, fold it over and over, fold it horizontally, then open it and fold it vertically, or score it. Scoring involves pressing lines firmly into the surface of the paper using the edge of a scissor blade. For this project, you can create curved folds by scoring *gentle* "c" curves or "s" curves onto a piece. These lines should all be parallel to each other. Then fan fold the piece using the scored lines. You can create any texture that does not involve cutting or piercing the paper. Once you have textured a piece, place it back in its proper place in its proper direction. Obviously, it will not fit, but you must know what goes where so that *you will not put the same two textures next to each other*. This is especially important when using crumbled pieces. Two fan folds can lie next to each other if they are folded in different directions. The greater the contrast between the textures of adjacent pieces, the more successful the project will be. A project could be done entirely in fan folds if all the neighboring pieces are folded in a different direction, but two crumbles can never lie next to each other. Stress this to the students.

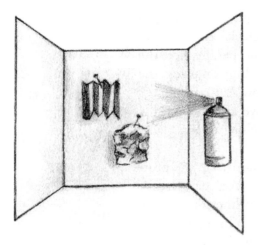

Once all the pieces are textured, you are ready for the next step, which is to spray paint them. This should be in a well-ventilated part of the room, perhaps near an open window. Place some newspaper or other protective covering on a table, and set up a large, tri-fold piece of cardboard on it.

I use the cartons that poster board comes in, which is a perfect configuration. Using straight pins, pin each piece of the design to the center section of the board, making sure that folds are oriented vertically and the numbers and name are on the back. If a piece is folded in two directions, you will spray it twice. Although there are many ways you can vary this process, for now you will be using inexpensive, black spray paint, matte or glossy. Holding the can at an *extremely raking angle*, spray each piece until the texture is permanent—that is, until the shadows are covered with dark paint. If a piece is folded

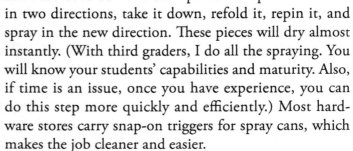

in two directions, take it down, refold it, repin it, and spray in the new direction. These pieces will dry almost instantly. (With third graders, I do all the spraying. You will know your students' capabilities and maturity. Also, if time is an issue, once you have experience, you can do this step more quickly and efficiently.) Most hardware stores carry snap-on triggers for spray cans, which makes the job cleaner and easier.

After spraying the pieces, it is time to glue them on to the background. Start with piece number one and go in the order of the numbers. Stress to the students that the pencil lines on the background paper are only there to show where a certain number goes, not to be matched by the pieces. The only thing that matters when gluing is that piece number 2 should fit perfectly next to piece number 1—there should be no gaps or overlaps. This may involve some flattening, especially with crumbled pieces. Place stick glue on the background paper in the area where piece one goes. Make sure piece 1 fits perfectly into its corner and flatten it over the glued area. Repeat the process with piece 2, making sure the edges of the two pieces fit as perfectly as possible.

Third graders Chloe Nusbaum and Kendall Baten completed this assignment very successfully, showing lots of contrast.

This project will take more than one period. When collecting these projects, I stack them and wrap the stack in a large piece of three-foot-wide roll paper. Newspaper taped together will work as well.

Lesson 8: Unity

A sense of oneness created from many different things

Lesson Summary: Students will create a monoprint using a sandpaper printing plate and crayons.

Purpose: Students will study unity and use several techniques to create a unified print to reinforce the concept.

Materials: #60 sandpaper, pencils, crayons, 12″ × 18″ construction paper in various colors and values, an iron, newspapers

Review: Texture, color schemes, repetition, relatedness

New Vocabulary/Concepts: Unity, monoprint

Time: Six periods

Possible Visual Aids: Works by Georges Seurat (although the theory is different, the textures are similar), real prints of some sort

---

Unity is a very hard principle to discuss because virtually every visual aid that involves great art displays it. You can't compare two pieces and say, "The one on the left shows unity and the one on the right doesn't." Unity is that quality of a work that makes all its parts seem to belong. Once again we will begin with a vocabulary lesson. Write the word "unity" on the board and ask if anyone can define it. If people offer definitions, discuss them and then underline "unit" and "uni" and ask for other words with this root or prefix. Be sure that, aside from words like "unicycle" and "unicorn," the list includes "union," "uniform," and "United States." Obviously, the word has something to do with one or oneness. What does a uniform do? It makes everyone—short or tall, blond or redhead, black or white, male or female—look like part of the same team. Even though Alaska and Florida have very different climates and cultures and geography, they are united by such things as government, language, and road systems into one country. Elaborate on this concept until the students understand that unity means bringing disparate things together to create one cohesive whole. When we look at a unified artwork, we don't see anything that looks as if it doesn't belong. This does not mean that nothing stands out—we have already discussed "emphasis," so we know that things are stressed in art all the time. It means that nothing stands out in a discordant or unacceptable way. Let's say I am dressed for a formal ball. I am wearing a long, beautiful gown, my hair and makeup are perfect, and I'm wearing high-top sneakers. Obviously, the emphasis will be on my feet, but not in a good way. Your reaction would be, "Why is she wearing those shoes?" Some works of art are made of incredibly diverse parts, but that very diversity becomes a unifying factor. It's only when you see something that makes you ask, "Why is that there?" or see something that distracts you from the point of the work, that you would judge a piece as lacking in unity.

There are many ways to create unity in a work of art. Repetition of any element, use of related shapes, great composition, color schemes, and so forth all help unify a piece.

After you have discussed unity at some length, demonstrate the project. This is a printmaking project, and it can be a little pricey because the printing plate is a full-sized sheet of 60-grade sandpaper. You might get these donated or have each student bring in one, if that is feasible for your population. I find it much more cost-effective to buy in bulk. Warn each student that they will only get one piece.

Hold your demonstration piece up on the board, and draw a shape with a pencil. Explain that you can't erase normally on sandpaper, but if you don't like something you have done, you can simply blow the pencil marks off. Demonstrate this by erasing your shape in this manner (which the students will think is very funny), but then warn them that this is good news and bad news. The good aspect is that erasing is easy—you simply shake or blow on the sandpaper. The bad aspect is that erasing is easy—you simply shake or blow on the sandpaper. That is, an unwary sneeze or jerking the sheet might destroy the design. It is vital to put one's name on the piece on the back before starting, and collecting and returning projects must be done delicately. Very small shapes will not work for this lesson, but compositions need not be tessellated. Shapes may float on negative space. Remind students that this is going to be a print, so anything they draw will come out reversed in the final step.

I don't like to waste sandpaper, so I use a different piece for the next step of the demo. Explain to the students that they will be using crayons and that they must select a color scheme. One of the main purposes of a color scheme is to create unity. In your coloring demonstration, you need only color a small area of your sandpaper, about three by three inches, so one piece can serve for several years. I like using yellows, reds, and oranges for my examples, and I always add shapes in gold and silver. Metallics work extremely well in this project. Explain to the students that they will be covering their entire sheet of sandpaper, but that you are only going to do enough to show them the process.

When using the crayon, color very heavily. You should see little or none of the sandpaper brown showing through. This is one of those situations where you will want to practice a few times before you present the project. In the demo, you might want to color one shape too lightly so that students will see what happens when the crayon is not thick enough. Place several shapes, approximately one by two or three inches, close together but not touching. When the students color their designs, they should stay off the pencil lines so that there is a *thin* space between each shape.

Step three involves an iron, which should be set fairly high. Once again, you will want to practice in advance. Put a pad of newspaper on a counter or table and place a piece of 12″ by 18″ construction paper on it. For my demo, I use black, because the effect of my reds, oranges, yellows, and metallics against that background is very dramatic. Center the sandpaper face down in the center of the construction paper, leaving a border of two or three inches. You could iron the back of the sandpaper, but I prefer to flip the pair over and iron on the back of the construction paper. If you do flip them over, try to keep the sandpaper centered. You will see the wax bleeding through, and after some practice, you will know when the transfer is complete. If you feel you have missed a space, you can carefully reregister the plate on the image and add more heat. The resulting print should have a beautiful texture that is similar if not identical over the entire surface. Be somewhat careful with metallics. They are softer than most crayons and can go on too heavily, causing puddles on the print. While this can be lovely in its own way, it can also cause the piece to lack unity.

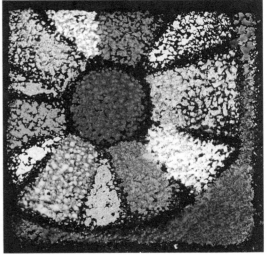

This project achieves unity in three ways. The color scheme, the related texture, and the underlying color of the paper creating a web of lines between the shapes and showing through the dots, all help unify the work.

You will want to have several pencils for each student, because they will wear down very quickly. You might also keep some larger boxes of crayons in the room for students who choose monochromatic color schemes. There are more intensities and values of colors in these sets. You will help each student choose his or her background paper based upon their color scheme. With dark colors, you should choose a light background, and vice versa. Black, light blue, light gray, and pale purple are some of my favorite choices. Older students could experiment with different effects and possibly do their own ironing. For younger children, of course, you will do this step. Once again, I urge you to experiment with this project yourself. You will find that white takes on various hues when printed and that you can mix crayons for interesting effects. Remember that black, white, gray, and metallics can be used with any color scheme, and caution the students to balance their colors and values. If the

The texture for the unity project should look something like this. (See color insert)

results of a print are disappointing, have the student recolor the area or areas that didn't print well, carefully realign the sandpaper face down on the *original* print and re-iron it. You can do this as often as needed.

After a few children have printed their pieces, you might want to discuss how prints are signed. This project results in a monoprint. Most printmaking techniques are designed to create a series of identical products. Monoprint techniques create one-of-a-kind results. No matter how many times this plate is reprinted (you can recolor and reprint the plate as often as you like), the results will never be exactly alike. Prints are always signed in pencil. The artist's name appears in cursive immediately under the lower-right-hand side of the image. The number of the print appears under the left-hand side. It is expressed in the form of a fraction. The denominator reflects the total number of prints that look exactly like this one. Runs can be very small or extremely large—as many as 2,500 to 5,000 or more. The smaller the run, the more valuable the print. The top number reflects the print's position in the series. For example, 7/250 on a work tells us that this piece was the seventh one printed in a series of 250. For a monoprint the symbol is 1/1—there is only one print that looks exactly like this one. Have each student sign his or her print accordingly.

Lesson 9: Movement and Rhythm

Movement: How our eye travels across the artwork
Rhythm: A strong, repeated pattern of elements

Lesson Summary: Students will create a Styrofoam plate print.

Purpose: The project will reinforce the concepts of rhythm and movement that have just been introduced.

Materials: 6″ × 9″ Styrofoam printing plates or grocery trays, pencils, water-based printing ink, spoons, 4″ soft rubber brayers, newspapers, 9″ × 12″ glass panes with taped edges, 12″ × 18″ manila paper, 8½″ × 11″ computer paper, paper towels

Review: Printing, signing, and numbering prints

New Vocabulary/Concepts: Rhythm, movement, brayer, intaglio (optional), bas relief (optional)

Time: Four+ periods, depending on how many prints a student does

Possible Visual Aids: Prints by Albrecht Durer, paintings by Mark Tobey or Jackson Pollack, quilt stories by Faith Ringgold

This project requires some fairly specialized equipment, including printer's ink and brayers. If you do not have access to these materials, you could probably create a similar lesson using large potatoes and tempera paint. If you have never done potato printing, there are several books and Web sites to help you.

Most students will already know the meaning of movement generally. In a work of art, it refers to how our eye is led across the picture or sculpture. Line is an element that has inherent movement, but our eye could follow a series of shapes or colors or textures or values or forms. Figure 1 has little or no movement, while Figure 2 has a lot. It will probably be sufficient to show some diagrams or visual aids to reinforce this concept and then move on to rhythm.

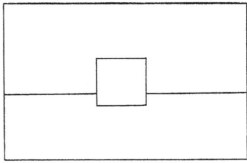

Figure 1

Rhythm is very closely related to pattern. Most of the children will be familiar with rhythm in music, so it is helpful to use this knowledge to help them understand the visual kind. Draw an image on the board that is similar to the one shown in Figure 3 and have the students interpret the rhythm by clapping their hands or tapping on the desks. You may repeat this exercise with similar drawings and/or visual aids until you feel the students get the idea.

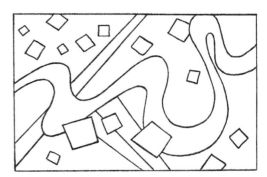

Figure 2

For this project, I use the 6″ by 9″ Styrofoam printing plates that you can order from virtually any art supply catalog. (They also come in 9″ by 12″.) If this does not fit your budget, start stockpiling the (cleaned) Styrofoam trays that supermarkets use for meats and produce. You will need one for each student, with a few extras for emergencies. If you use these, simply have the children remove the curved up edges using scissors. Warn them not to take off too much of the flat center part, but anything that sticks up must be removed. Then lay a ruler close to the edge and pull a very sharp pencil along the outside of the ruler again and again until the excess falls off and the edges of the printing

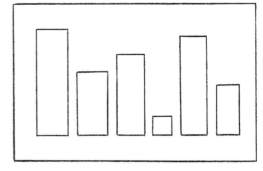

Figure 3

plate are smooth and straight. Children can lightly incise their names on the back.

To print your plate, you will need water-based printing ink, a piece of glass about 9″ by 12″, computer paper, manila, a spoon, a soft rubber brayer, and some newspaper. You will need to duplicate these materials at every printing station you set up for the students, although if the stations are near each other students can share ink. The more printing stations, the faster the project will go and the more prints each student will be able to make. Depending on the arrangement of your room, you can place these stations on desks or counters or at a special table. I have four or five stations for a class of 20.

Before you begin your demonstration, set up a printing station. Open a full sheet of newspaper and place it in a spot where everyone can see. Tape the edges of the glass so that no one can get cut, and place the glass on one half of the newspaper. Printing ink comes in jars or tubes. (I find jars more economical, because you can put unused ink back.) This ink comes in various colors, and you might put a different color at each station, although if you are using white paper, the darker colors and black are best. An interesting effect is to use white paint on black paper. Construction paper is OK, but thinner paper prints more easily. If you use ink in a jar, place a jar and a spoon (plastic is fine) on the newspaper, and place your Styrofoam plate and a pencil nearby, so that it is ready for your demo. If you are using grocery trays, start by showing the students how to prepare the edges.

The nice thing about this printing surface is that the students can engrave their images on it using only a sharp pencil. For a crisp, smooth line, hold the pencil at an angle and pull it in the direction of the eraser. Don't push the pencil. Surprisingly, the Styrofoam has a grain, and the pencil will move in some directions more easily that others. Your line should be incised about halfway through the Styrofoam. If you press too hard, the line will go all the way through the plate and possibly break it. If your lines are too shallow, they will fill with ink and not show when you print.

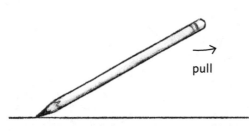

pull

For your demonstration, you can simply draw a simple abstract. You want as much movement as possible. Usually, the more movement, the more rhythm. Remind the students that the element line has great movement, but they can also achieve movement by using several shapes. Be careful with the plate—don't dent it with knuckles or put lines so close together that an area is depressed. You can draw a picture, but remember that the purpose of the image is to display movement and rhythm, and abstracts frequently work better for this.

Once the image is incised, lay it on the empty side of the newspaper. While your hands are clean, take a piece of 12″ by 18″ manila and a piece of 8½″ by 11″ computer paper and set them aside. Explain to the students that they will each put this setup at their desk with clean hands before going to a printing station. Have the stacks of paper easily accessible.

Place about three-fourths of a teaspoonful of ink on the glass and spread it with the brayer until the roller is fully covered. Explain that the purpose of rolling the brayer through the ink is to coat the brayer, not to spread the ink all over the glass. You don't need to press hard with the brayer, as that will simply push the ink around. If you need more ink, add it to the glass, but don't put too much out. You don't want gloppy ink on your brayer. Once the brayer is evenly coated, roll it gently over the surface of the plate, going in various directions until the surface is completely covered.

Pick the plate up carefully by the very edges with your fingertips and turn it upside down over the computer paper. Center it as much as possible before lowering it onto the paper. Give it a small tap, so that the plate sticks to the paper, then pick the paper up by the corner and turn the pair over onto the manila. The purpose of the manila is to keep the front of the print clean. Using the palm of your hand, rub firmly over the back of the paper, making sure you rub the entire area, especially the edges. Don't do this too long or too hard. Turn the paper so that it is in the portrait position. Place one hand on the lower part of the paper and plate, and with the other hand, carefully and slowly peel the print back from the top of the plate. Don't pull the print from the corner. The result should be solid except for the incised lines. The border should be very clean, not full of inky fingerprints.

If a student is reprinting with the same ink, there is no need to rinse the plate between prints. If he is changing colors, or if the plate needs work, like deepening a line, he can rinse the plate carefully and blot it dry. Hands should be clean when setting up papers at the desk. Prints should not be signed and numbered until totally dry. (See the previous lesson.) Students can place a number on the back of the paper in pencil before printing to keep the run straight. I usually try for a total run of five in this project, although it might take many more tries than that to get five good results.

This project creates a good opportunity to discuss printmaking in general. This is essentially an intaglio printing plate, but it is printed like a bas relief. Etchings are intaglio. The ink is usually pushed down into the lines and wiped from the surface, so only the lines print. A woodcut is a bas relief. The ink is applied to the surface and the cut-away parts don't print. Depending on your circumstances and knowledge of printmaking, you might want to elaborate on these concepts.

Lesson 10: Comparing and Contrasting Artworks

I usually use this lesson not only to reinforce art vocabulary (see the final lessons in First and Second Years) but also to prepare students a bit for their upcoming study of art history. I try to choose three works with very different approaches. One is Nonobjective Formalist, such as a later work by Piet Mondrian. One is Abstract Expressionistic, such as a painting by Wasily Kandinsky or Jackson Pollack. And one is simply Realistic, perhaps something like Francisco Goya's *Don Manuel Osorio*, or possibly a more imaginative realism, like works by Henri Rousseau. You can use virtually any visual aids that serve your purpose.

Bibliography

Anderson, R. L. 1990. *Calliope's Sisters: A Comparative Study of Philosophies of Art.* Englewood Cliffs, NJ: Prentice Hall.

Borten, Helen. 1961. *A Picture Has a Special Look.* Eau Claire, WI: E. M. Hale.

Carle, E. 1998. *Hello Red Fox.* New York: Simon and Schuster.

Coerr, Eleanor. 1993. *Sadako and the Thousand Cranes.* New York: G. P. Putnam's Sons.

Livo, Norma, ed. *Joining In: An Anthology of Audience Participation Stories and How to Tell Them.* Cambridge, MA: Yellow Moon Press.

Resources

Materials and Visual Aids

Dick Blick Art Materials, P.O. Box 1267, Galesburg, IL 61402-1267, 800-621-8293, www.dickblick.com

Nasco Arts and Crafts, 901 Janesville Ave., Fort Atkinson, WI 53538 *or* P.O. Box 3837, Modesto, CA 95352, 800-558-9595, www.enasco.com

Sax Arts and Crafts, 2725 S. Moorland Rd., New Berlin, WI 53151, 800-558-6696, www.artsupplies.com

Triarco Arts and Crafts, 2600 Fernbrook Lane, Suite 100, North Plymouth, MN 55447, 800-328-3360, www.triarcoarts.com

United Art and Education (Art Materials Catalog), P.O. Box 9219, Fort Wayne, IN 46899, 800-322-3247, www.UnitedNow.com

University Prints, 37 Cottage St., Sanford, ME 04073, 207-490-6977, www.uni-prints.com

Magazines

Arts and Activities, 12345 World Trade Drive, San Diego, CA 92128, www.artsand
activities.com

Scholastic, Inc. (Art), 557 Broadway, New York, NY 10012, 800-387-1437 ext. 99, www.scholastic.com

School Arts, 50 Portland St., Worcester, MA 01608, 800-533-2847, www.davis-art.com (go to *School Arts* magazine)

Index

performing arts, judging, 12

pigments versus light, 46

plus (+) sign, meaning of, 19

portfolio, creating in grade one, 19–20

poses, determining for emphasis lesson, 168

positive versus negative
    shapes, 131–133
    space, 31

poster board, creating shapes from, 70–72

Prescott, Luke, 162

primaries
    creating tertiaries from, 105
    examples of, 26
    mixing, 104–105
    sets of, 5

printing, 30

printing station, setting up, 178

prints, signing, 176

procedures, demonstration of, 5–6

projector, using to review color theory, 103

projects
    collecting and passing back, 7
    mounting, 11
    preparing for, 5
    starting with pencils, 9–10

puppets, creating from paper bags, 97–98

pyramid shape, description of, 90

R

radial balance
    definition of, 159–162
    using, 159–162

reality, drawing from, 10

rectangular prism, description of, 90

relationships, applying to shapes, 77

repetition, stimulating memory with, 6

rhythm and movement lesson, 176–179

room arrangement, planning, 2

rules for art class, explaining, 4–5

S

sandpaper, using in unity lesson, 173–176

scale painting, technique for, 52

secondary colors, examples of, 26

second-year curriculum
    color schemes, analogous, 116–118, complementary, 112–114, introduction, 108–110, monochromatic, 110–112, triadic, 114–116
    color, intermediate, 104–105, 106–107, mixing primaries, 104–105, review, 102–103, tertiary colors, 104–105, 106–107
    contrast and compare, 146
    creating a portfolio, 101
    distortion, 133–136
    file and free, 108, 118, 124, 130, 138, 142
    form, 143–145, organic, 145–146, review, 143
    line, calligraphic, 140–142, creating the illusion of form, 139–140, review, 139–140
    pattern, relationship to texture, 128–130
    shade, 123–124
    shape, negative, 131–133, positive, 131–133, review, 131
    tessellations, 137–138
    texture, of the medium, 125–128, relationship to pattern, 128–130, review, 125–126
    tint, 123–124
    value, 3–d effects, 120–123, as shade, 123–124, as tint, 123–124, review, 119–120
    watercolors, 106–107

self-esteem, considering, 15–16

self-portraits, creating in emphasis lesson, 168–169

shade, definition of, 50. *See also* tint and shade

shapes
    of clouds, 79–80
    creating, 70–72
    definition of, 70
    distorting, 133–136
    irregular and organic types of, 74–76
    positive versus negative types of, 131–133

relationships between, 76–78

"Specials" teachers, grading system for, 15

spring picture, creating, 80

Steinbart, Peter, 165, 169

still life, creating, 88–89

student work
    displaying, 10–12
    judging, 12–17
    touching, 8–9

students, slower and faster types of, 9

styrofoam printing plates, using, 177–179

supplies, including in baskets, 2. *See also* materials

symmetrical designs, creating, 28

symmetry
    versus balance, 157–158
    definition of, 156–157

T

tables, using, 2

tagboard, using to create portfolios, 20

teeter-totter, considering as lever, 157

templates, using with shapes, 121–122

tertiaries
    creating, 33–35
    creating from primaries, 105
    and intermediaries, 106–107

tessellations
    creating, 137–138
    definition of, 60

tests
    administering for third year, 148–150
    answer key for, 151–152
    giving, 8

texture
    definition of, 57
    versus form, 63
    versus pattern, 64–67, 128–130
    with special look, 67–69
    using, 125–126
    and watercolor resist crumble, 125–128

texture illusion draw and fill project, creating, 59–61

third-year curriculum

balance, formal, 156–159, informal, 162–166, introduction, 156–159, radial, 159–162

color, review, 151–155, wheel, 153

comparing and contrasting artworks, 179–180

contrast, 166–170, 170–172

creating a portfolio, 151

crossword puzzle, 154

distortion, 166–170

movement, 176–179

review test, 147, 148–150, 151

rhythm, 176–179

symmetry, 156–159

unity, 173–176

value, review, 151–155

3-D effects, creating with charcoal values, 120–123

tint and shade. *See also* shade
    values as, 123–124
    working with, 49–51

trees, drawing in grade-one curriculum, 21–22. *See also* fall trees

triadic color schemes, working with, 114–116

triangular prism, description of, 90

U

unity, creating, 173–176

V

value collage, creating, 53

values
    definition of, 44, 47–48
    as property of color, 51–53
    referring to, 119–120
    reviewing in second year, 119–120
    reviewing in third year, 151–155
    as tint and shade, 123–124

visual aids
    analogous color schemes, 117
    for artists' uniqueness, 21
    for balance, formal balance, and symmetry, 156
    black and white on colored paper, 49
    for black crayon on white paper, 47
    for calligraphic lines and symmetry, 86

for charcoal value 3-D effects, 121
for clay, 96
for color mixing with watercolors, 106
for color schemes, 108
for complementary color schemes, 112
for contrast and compare, 146
for contrast lesson in third year, 170
for contrasting and comparing
    artworks, 98
for creating calligraphic lines, 141
for creating Captain's Shirt form, 93
for creating coloring book, 84
for creating lines, 81
for creating paper bag puppets, 97
for creating portfolio, 19
for creating shapes, 71
for creating spring picture, 80
for creating tertiaries, 33
cut paper complementary colors, 40
for distortion, 133
for drawing with "Chunk-o-Crayon,"
    32
for emphasis through distortion and
    contrast, 166
for form, 90
for form and paper houses, 143
for geometric shapes, 72
for informal balance, 163
for irregular and organic shapes, 75
keeping on display, 3
line used to create illusion of form,
    139
for lines as directions, 83
for mixing primaries, 104
for monochromatic color schemes, 110
for movement and rhythm lesson, 177
for organic form sculpture, 145
for paper fold and crumble montage,
    62
for paper weaving, 64
for positive and negative shapes, 131
for radial balance, 160
for related shapes, 76
resources for, 182

for still life, 89
for tessellations, 137
for texture, 58
for texture and watercolor resist
    crumble, 125
for texture illusion draw and fill, 60
for texture versus pattern, 128
for texture with special look, 67
for triadic color schemes, 114
for unity lesson in third year, 173
for value as tint and shade, 123
for value collage, 53
for value review, 119
for watercolor fingerprints, 51
for watercolor painting, 30
for winter picture, 55
visual arts, judging, 12
vocabulary, development of, xii

W

warm versus cool primaries, 5
washes, creating, 29–30
water, providing for projects, 2–3
watercolor fingerprints, creating, 51–53
watercolor paintings, creating, 30–31
watercolors
    choosing for watercolor resist
        crumble, 126–127
    color mixing with, 106–107
    using with value as tint and shade,
        124
weaving, patterns in, 66
websites
    Captain's Shirt, 94
    Crayola crayons, 115
    materials and visual aids, 182
weight, creating in works of art,
    156–157
white chalk, using, 50
white construction paper, using, 52
white light, explanation of, 45
winter picture, creating, 55
words. *See* vocabulary
works of art. *See* artworks